Practical Risk Assessment for Project Management

WILEY SERIES IN
SOFTWARE ENGINEERING PRACTICE

Series Editors:

Patrick A.V. Hall, *The Open University, UK*
Martyn A. Ould, *Praxis Systems plc, UK*
William E. Riddle, *Software Design & Analysis, Inc., USA*

Aims and Scope

The focus of this series is the software creation and evolution processes and related organisational and automated systems necessary to support them. The aims is to produce books dealing with all aspects of software engineering, particularly the practical exploitation of the best methods and tools for the development process.

The series covers the following topics:

- process models and software lifecycle

- project management, quality assurance, configuration management, process and product standards

- the external business environment and legal constraints

- computer aided software engineering (CASE) and integrated project support environments (IPSES)

- requirements analysis, specification and validation

- architectural design techniques, software components and re-use

- system design methods and verification

- system implementation, build and test

- maintenance and enhancement

For a full list of titles in this series, see back pages.

PRACTICAL RISK ASSESSMENT FOR PROJECT MANAGEMENT

Stephen Grey

ICL, UK

JOHN WILEY & SONS

Chichester • New York • Brisbane • Toronto • Singapore

Copyright © 1995 by John Wiley & Sons Ltd
Baffins Lane, Chichester
West Sussex PO19 1UD, England
National Chichester (01243) 779777
International +44 1243 779777

Other Wiley Editorial Offices

John Wiley & Sons, Inc., 605 Third Avenue,
New York, NY 10158-0012, USA

Jacaranda Wiley Ltd, 33 Park Road, Milton,
Queensland 4064, Australia

John Wiley & Sons (Canada) Ltd, 22 Worcester Road,
Rexdale, Ontario M9W 1L1, Canada

John Wiley & Sons (SEA) Pte Ltd, 37 Jalan Pemimpin #05-04,
Block B, Union Industrial Building, Singapore 2057

Library of Congress Cataloging-in-Publication Data
Grey, Stephen.
    Risk analysis for IT projects / Stephen Grey.
        p.   cm. — (Wiley series in software engineering practice)
    Includes bibliographical references (p.   ) and index.
    ISBN 0 471 93979 X : $36.00
    1. Information technology.   2. Risk assessment.   I. Title.
    II. Series.
    T58.5.G74   1995
    005.1′068′4—dc20   94-46422
                                                        CIP

British Library Cataloguing in Publication Data
A catalogue record for this book is available from the British Library

ISBN 0 471 93979 X

Typeset in 10/12pt Palatino from authors' disk by MHL Typesetting Ltd, Coventry
Printed and bound in Great Britain by Biddles Ltd, Guildford and King's Lynn

CONTENTS

INTRODUCTION

This book describes how to make quantitative assessments of the uncertainty affecting cost, schedule and revenue estimates in a project-based business. Understanding the uncertainty in estimates, and being able to set achievable but competitive targets and commitments, goes to the heart of many of the major decisions affecting risk in a projects business.

It would be a mistake to presume that quantitative assessment is all you need to know about project risk management, though, and this introduction is intended to put the rest of the book in context. It explains where quantitative assessments fit within the wider field of risk management, and sketches out that wider field for the reader.

RISK MANAGEMENT OVERVIEW

Risk management is a very broad topic. It is entirely a matter of choice where you draw the line between project risk management and general project management, or even whether you do separate them at all. Three views of the relationship between risk management and project management are illustrated in Figures 1–3. They are all perfectly valid, and each one might be a useful way of thinking about the subject in different circumstances.

Figure 1 is the traditional view of risk management, a part of the project management function, carried out by the project manager or delegated to a member of his or her team. Figure 2 is almost the opposite. It is based on the idea that if there was no risk in a project the need for project management would fade away, it would become an administrative task. Put another way, the main purpose of project management is to

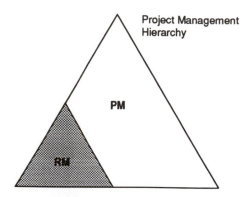

Figure 1 Risk management supporting project management

manage the risks in a project. This view is sometimes summed up in the term 'Risk-driven project management'.

The third view, in Figure 3, is closer to the picture of risk management set out in the rest of this introduction. It illustrates the fact that risk management has to be considered in all aspects of project management, but there are also some tasks which most project managers would expect to delegate to consultants or external specialists.

Figures 1–3 are concerned with separating out the parts of project management we choose to classify as risk management. The labels given to functions make little difference to what people do, but they can help us think and plan clearly. Before going into the process of risk management in

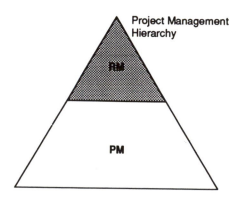

Figure 2 Risk management is *raison d'être* of project management

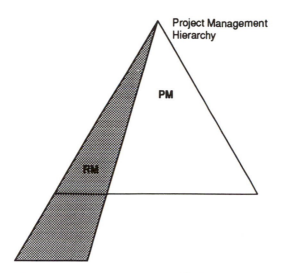

Project Management
Hierarchy

PM

RM

Figure 3 Risk management permeates all of project management

more detail, it is worth clarifying a few other labels, dealing with what might be called the lifecycle or lifetime of a risk.

Figure 4 shows some of the major stages between recognising that a risk might affect a project and reaching a point where the matter requires no further attention. This picture illustrates several terms which are used when describing the overall risk management process. The key parts are:

- identification of an issue which could jeopardise the success of a project;
- assessment of that issue, following which it might be rejected as insignificant, or if it is significant it might be referred up or down in the management structure;
- for any remaining risks, containment plans to be added to the main plan and contingency plans to be invoked if containment fails; associated with containment and contingency plans are two control mechanisms, monitoring and control measures for the containment plans and a trigger for the contingency plan.

This diagram simply describes something we all do every day, mostly without thinking about it. Difficulties arise when risks are hard to identify and assess because the work is unfamiliar or complex. When this happens it can be useful to have an explicit process to follow, so you can take it a step at a time, in manageable pieces.

The terms set out in Figure 4 are used to describe the overall risk management process in the next section.

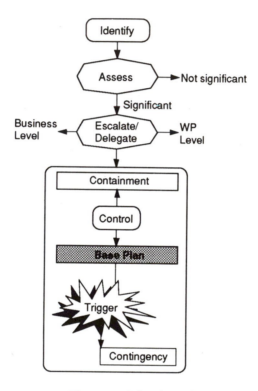

Figure 4 Life of a risk

Risk Management Process Outline

This outline is based on the sequence in which the key stages of risk management are addressed. It is not the only way to describe risk management, but it is useful and easy to follow.

Nine steps are used to describe the process, as follows:

- identifying stakeholders
- identifying key success measures

- isolating the baseline project plan
- identifying issues placing success at risk
- assessing the issues' likelihood and potential impact
- assigning ownership
- risk management planning
- aggregate analysis
- monitoring and reviewing.

Stakeholders

Risks are the issues which might keep a project from being a success. Everyone concerned with a project will want something slightly different from it, so the first step in risk management must be to identify whose views matter, which stakeholders you are concerned with.

This step is rarely given explicit attention. Sometimes it is so obvious it needs none, but even in simple cases, confusion between customer and supplier viewpoints can muddy the waters. Differences between the priorities of users and IT departments are even easier to neglect, and are capable of generating just as much confusion.

Success measures

The only way to be sure what a particular stakeholder regards as success is to ask them; assumptions are often misleading. However, many people find it difficult to summarise their objectives clearly and might need help to define what for them represents success.

Where success measures are left unclear, issues will be raised as risks which no one who matters really cares about, and important risks can be overlooked. Both types of mistake undermine the cost-effectiveness of the risk management process, wasting effort and time.

Suppliers are generally concerned about money, and customers are focused on timescales, performance and quality, but things are rarely that simple. For instance, is it the overall profitability of the project, the cash flow by year end or the next quarter's revenue which will drive decision-making for the supplier? Is the customer concerned with the date of final acceptance, achieving an interim operating capability, or each of a string of intermediate milestones?

As businesses enter into more and more partnerships and risk sharing ventures for the provision of IT services, the success measures of customers and suppliers are bound to overlap more than they have in the past. Differences will remain, though, between and within organisations, and if they are not clearly understood they will lead to confusion.

Baseline plans

Risks only make sense in the context of a plan. If you believe there are risks associated with achieving your objectives you must have some idea how you propose to achieve those objectives, otherwise there is no reason to think they will not be achieved.

A plan need not be documented and formally structured, but analysis is obviously easier with a plan on paper. For the analysis of IT projects, three types of information are required:

- a description of what is to be delivered, including a schematic system outline;
- the resource and management structure of the project;
- an activity plan, in the form of a Gantt or PERT chart.

Depending on the nature of the work and the commercial environment in which it is to be pursued, details of the contract, subcontracts and other agreements or policies affecting the project might have to be understood as well.

Having assured access to the plans for a project, it is important to extract a suitable summary view of them. It is rarely cost-effective to carry out a risk assessment at the finest level of detail used in a plan; choosing a suitable view of a project for analysis is the key to containing the effort it absorbs.

Risk issues

Simply identifying potential risks is becoming increasingly difficult. Part of the reason for this is the pace of technological and commercial change, combining with devolution of responsibility and empowerment, leading to more and more complex systems being implemented by people with relatively less and less experience. They might be experienced in something, but if this week's project includes a novel development, no one will have a track record of handling it. There is a substantial need for help with identifying risks.

Since risks are inherently unpredictable, identifying them is a creative, brainstorming activity. Support for brainstorming has to strike a difficult balance. On the one hand, it is important to draw attention to known issues, the standard risks which must be considered, and stimulate thoughts about new ones. On the other hand, very specific checklists can focus attention so closely on yesterday's problems that issues arising from novel technology or new working practices are overlooked.

The identification of risks carries on throughout the life of a project, of course, but there will usually be a concerted exercise at the outset which aims to break the back of it. This might be based on the private work of an individual, interviews by consultants, group workshops or any combination of these mechanisms. The aim of this step is to raise issues for consideration. As with any brainstorming exercise, assessment or evaluation is best deferred, to avoid stifling the creative process.

Assessment

The issues raised in the previous step will span a range of likelihoods and impacts. They will include some risks which would sink the project and some which would almost pass unnoticed, some which are very likely to arise and some which are almost certain not to arise. The resources devoted to containing a risk, and the provision for contingency action, will obviously depend on these two characteristics, likelihood and impact.

If planners and decision makers are clear in their own minds about the level of resources to assign to managing each risk, the assessment might go no further than the private thoughts of these people. Where matters are not so clear, or the resource allocations have to be justified to others, something more formal is usually required.

Formal risk assessment can range from simple classification into categories such as High, Medium and Low, through to the use of mathematical models as described in the rest of this book. The amount of effort devoted to assessing risks can vary a lot, but the general rule is to use as little as is necessary to arrive at reliable planning decisions. This is the first place where the techniques described in the rest of the book can be applied. They can be used to arrive at rational assessments of the significance of risks where subjective and qualitative methods are insufficient.

Once you have decided which risks are significant, there is still a question about the level at which they should be handled. Some of the larger problems affecting a project might have to be tackled by the business, problems which affect a group of related projects or are so large that they dwarf a single project's finances. Others will fall naturally into an allocated work package and will not need the long-term attention of the project manager.

Ownership

Each risk will have containment and contingency plans associated with it. As with any other part of a project, responsibility for plans has to be assigned to a named individual. Ownership of risks cannot be shared because ownership of actions cannot be shared, and clear assignment of ownership is obviously crucial to ensuring that risk management plans are properly addressed.

Some customers expect suppliers to relieve them of all risks, even though it might cost the supplier more to manage certain risks than it would the customer, and these costs are bound to be reflected in the supplier's price. The fact that it is often more cost-effective for customers to manage the risks which they can control than to pay a supplier to take them, has yet to penetrate some purchasers' consciousness.

Planning

There are two ways to respond to the possibility that an activity might drift or even jump out of control. You can do something before and during the activity to keep it in line (containment action) and you can be prepared to pull the work back into line if control fails (contingency action).

Containment can be achieved by:

- understanding the uncertainty better, so it becomes easier to control;
- changing the approach to an activity so it is more likely to succeed;
- applying extra effort or other resources to the existing approach.

All these mean committing oneself to do something, possibly spend more money, in the hope that the work will be more likely to stay on track. Containment plans describe something which will happen, something you have decided you will do.

Contingency plans are different; they might not happen. Contingency plans are probably the most familiar face of risk management, the steps you will take when things go wrong.

Containment and contingency plans both need control mechanisms. To ensure that a containment plan achieves its aims there must be a means of monitoring its performance and modifying the intensity of the action. If it is not working, more effort might be necessary. If it is working well you might be able to turn it down and save money. Monitoring mechanisms might already be in place, as part of the standard project management infrastructure. Quite often, though, thinking about how to control a containment measure will show that a project needs an extra monitor to keep it on target.

To ensure that contingency plans are effective, it is vital to be clear what will trigger them, under what conditions you will decide that containment has failed. If this is not spelled out in advance, the natural tendency to hope that things will improve can lead to a project drifting beyond the latest date when the contingency plan could have avoided a schedule slip.

Once risk management plans have been prepared, containment actions will be absorbed into the basic plan for the project. For presentation purposes the containment plans might be described separately, but there can only be one project plan, and that will include the containment plans.

Aggregation

When all the major risks are exposed and plans are in place to deal with them, the job is not over. Someone still has to decide what targets to set for the completion date and the cost budget. This is the second place where the techniques described in the rest of the book can be used.

By describing the uncertainty in the component parts of a project, the work package costs and the activity durations, and building these into models of the overall cost and duration, it is possible to calculate the range of realistically likely total costs and durations which might arise. It is also possible to find where, within those ranges, realistically achievable targets lie. This is an invaluable aid to two of the most crucial decisions affecting a project: the commitments on the budget and the end date.

Monitoring and reviewing

Monitoring and reviewing risk management plans are no different to monitoring and reviewing any other plans. They should form part of the routine project control mechanisms. The only aspect which might appear a little different is keeping a lookout for contingency plans which should be invoked. This is similar to a milestone check, though; it comes down to asking if something has happened or not.

MODELLING AND ASSESSMENT SUMMARY

Risk modelling is a powerful but simple technique which has an important role to play in two parts of the overall risk management process. When individual risks are assessed, models can be used to bring several uncertainties that make up a single risk together in one place, and produce a clear summary view of the danger to the project.

The most powerful role for risk modelling is in the assessment of overall project cost and schedule targets, understanding the uncertainty affecting them and ensuring that they are set at realistically achievable levels. That is the main subject of this book. The same techniques can easily be applied to headcounts, cash flows and other features of a projects business, but cost and schedule targets offer the biggest payoff for the least effort.

ACKNOWLEDGEMENTS

The contents of this book, and my ability to make what sense of them I can, owe a lot to: ICL, where the techniques described were refined and proven; the Association of Project Managers' Specific Interest Group on Project Risk Management, whose members provided technical input and valuable opinions on working methods; and my father, who taught me by example that even relatively abstract matters can be understood if you can get past the initial tendency to believe that they are beyond comprehension.

1

PROJECT RISK ASSESSMENT

1.1 RISK IN A PROJECT BUSINESS

Project working is rapidly gaining acceptance as the most effective management approach for meeting short- and medium-term objectives. Trends towards individual empowerment and flatter organisations are pushing the responsibility for these projects further down the management hierarchy every year. With competition becoming increasingly fierce all the time, larger and larger risks are being shouldered by smaller and smaller organisations and even individuals.

As if the structural changes in business were not enough, the daily march of technology ensures that we are constantly faced with unfamiliar issues and increasing complexity. There is no modern day equivalent of the craftsman who becomes progressively more expert in a narrow field over his entire life. Individuals and organisations have to absorb new technology and ways of doing business all the time. No one has the luxury of getting to know a task so well that it holds no surprises, and surprises mean risk.

Three areas of a project business crystallise most of our concerns about risk:

- price setting

- commitment to completion dates

- forecasting future levels of activity.

There is more to risk than this but these are the three areas which cause the greatest concern. These are the topics addressed by this book.

Price setting is always a tug of war between being competitive enough to get the work and the avoidance of losses. Price setting decisions are usually taken in a hurry, with uncertain cost estimates. Pressure to secure orders injects emotional and personal factors into the process, undermining rational assessment of this uncertainty and the risk it entails.

All the issues that afflict price setting apply equally to commitments on delivery dates. Most customers will ask for a tight schedule, and if anyone offers an even earlier date their bid will look very attractive, at first sight. This has to be balanced by the bidders against the damages and possibly penalties to be paid if the commitment is not honoured. Schedules are even more difficult to estimate reliably than costs, because, as well as the uncertainty in the component estimates, you have to allow for the logical dependencies between activities.

If we now move up a level from individual projects to the business as a whole, the same issues arise in a different form. Each business manager has to forecast a level of activity for the coming year, commit him or herself to achieving a certain revenue and profit, and invest in the staff and other resources required to make it happen. It is notoriously difficult to forecast the value of business likely to be won in a project environment. As well as being uncertain of which opportunities you will win or lose, you have to accept the customer's right to vary the work content, and so also the value of each prospect up to the last minute. On top of all that, it is quite common for internal factors to cause a customer to delay the start of a contract, and once work has started progress towards payment points might not be as fast as you had hoped.

Whether we are dealing with one project's cost and schedule or the future of an entire business, two things are constant.

- Somewhere in the process one or more individuals have a personal stake in the outcome, usually financial.

- Even small- and medium-sized projects and businesses present us with more uncertainty than an unaided human being can reliably assess.

Projects businesses need simple techniques to allow individuals to assess the risks they face, and help them make reliable decisions about commitments and targets. The information required to do this is often already at hand. Most people waste it. This book will show you how to harness this resource to improve the quality of your forecasting and decision-making.

The adage 'you can't manage what you can't measure' applies at least as much to risk as to anything else. Sometimes you can get the measure of an issue directly when it is simple, familiar and recurs regularly. You understand it intuitively and trust your judgement to take appropriate action. Most project risks are not like that, though. This book will take you through quantitative techniques that allow you to derive simple numerical measures of the uncertainty that you face.

Stories of project failures abound, but one of the most common general failings is to start with an inadequate budget or impossible schedule. There are innumerable reasons why this might happen, of course, and large amounts of effort are devoted to making sure that estimates and plans are realistic and achievable. Most of this effort is directed at making sure you leave nothing out, and trying to use the lessons of the past to get it right next time.

No matter how hard we work at formal methods, estimating metrics and checklists, we can never eliminate uncertainty and risk. In an ideal world there would always be plenty of time to prepare plans, but in reality plans are often put together in a rush. Even with lots of time, though, the fact that a project is always something of a one-off will ensure that planners and estimators need to deal with uncertainty. The only way to be sure of what is involved in a new task is to do it, so bids are always based on incomplete information.

This simple fact, that no matter how hard we work we can never remove the uncertainty from planning and estimating, is not widely understood. Our education system never says it in so many words, but the sciences in particular imply that if we only work away at something long enough it will be possible to tie it down as accurately as we want. In the real world this is not true. We have to live with uncertainty and the risk it causes. We have no choice.

We need a technique to understand the risks we face and to be able to make realistic commitments. This can be a matter of survival, but even if you are surviving and expect to continue doing so, risk can have a marked effect on your cost-effectiveness.

An organisation that habitually runs little risk will tend to be taking it easy. Low risk means low pressure and no incentive to pull out the stops. Conversely, an organisation that takes excessive risk will always be on the brink of failure. If it does survive it will only be by virtue of a lot of very hard work and uncontrollable luck. This can promote efficiency, but if it is taken too far too often staff will start to expect things to go wrong. Once that happens it is a small step to people feeling that matters are beyond their control and giving up.

There is an optimum level of risk which is high enough to encourage efficiency but low enough to let staff believe they have a chance. No one can write an equation for this optimum. It is now and is likely to remain a matter of judgement. The techniques set out in this book allow you to assess the risk you are taking and help you home in on your own optimum. They can help you to ensure that your projects start life with a fighting chance, in spite of the uncertainty and complexity in them.

1.2 RISK ASSESSMENT TECHNIQUES

Almost every book on project management mentions risk. Some do little more than mention it, whereas others go on at length. On the whole there is as much confusion in the literature on project risk as confusion caused by risk in the real world.

Methods of assessing risk broadly fall into three groups:

- issue-based methods, which ask you to think about technical, commercial, management and other types of risk; or else give you a checklist of things that might go wrong

- scoring techniques based on a questionnaire; this asks you if a certain factor is applicable to your project and assigns the project points, depending how bad it is, with the total number of points as a measure of the overall riskiness of the project.

- quantitative techniques which aim to represent the likelihood and impact of risks in terms of the usual planning measures, such as time and money.

Some methods are a mixture of all these approaches.

Before explaining the key points of each approach, it is worth thinking about the purpose of risk analysis. Its main objectives can be summarised in the following four points.

- Timeliness: above all else risk analysis must help you to identify issues while there is still time to deal with them.

- Priorities: having identified the risks to your project, you will usually have insufficient time or resources to address them all; so the next requirement is to help you to assign realistic priorities.

| | ASSESSMENT TYPE | | |
OBJECTIVE	Issue-based	Scoring	Quantitative
• Timeliness	Depends when applied	Depends when applied	Depends when applied
• Priorities	Little help	Some assessment	Quantitative measures of priority
• Aggregation	No help	Little help	Simple rational aggregation
• Decision Support	No help with commitments	Little help with commitments	Describes relationship between level of commitment and level of risk

Figure 1.1 Comparison of methods of risk assessment against objectives

- Aggregation: when you are making decisions about a project as a whole, such as what price to charge or when it can be delivered, you need to understand the overall level of risk it represents; so the next requirement is for risk analysis to help you aggregate several individual issues into a measure of overall risk.

- Decision support: finally, the heart of the whole process is decision-making, and risk analysis must produce information in a form which helps the decision-makers.

The ability of each type of technique to achieve these four objectives is summarised in Figure 1.1.

1.2.1 Issue-based techniques

Issue-based techniques make sure that you do not forget anything obvious. Some start with an assertion that all risks can be classified under a set of headings, such as:

- technical

- commercial

- internal

- external.

The idea is that you think about your project and the headings, and see if any problems spring to mind. This is a useful first step in risk assessment, but some methods go no further.

Instead of (or perhaps as well as) a set of headings to start you thinking, this type of approach might present you with a checklist. The checklist will usually represent yesterday's mistakes, the issues which caught you out last time. There is nothing wrong with that, of course. All that any of us has to go on is experience, and checklists can give you access to the experience of others, so you need not repeat their mistakes. A typical checklist for software development might prompt questions such as:

- is the development team familiar with the environment to be used?

- are two or more separate groups developing different parts of this software?

- will the system include any off-the-shelf packages?

Systems integration would be assessed with a different checklist and building works with another. There is no hard and fast rule about the size of a checklist, but they seem to run out at a few tens of items.

Checklists and related methods are useful memory joggers, but they have two big shortcomings. Firstly, they tend to be seen as exhaustive, giving people a false sense of security. It is tempting to think that if you have worked through the checklist nothing else can go wrong. Secondly, they are little help in assessing the overall level of risk represented by a project, or in determining realistic target budgets and timescales.

1.2.2 Scoring techniques

Scoring techniques are a natural extension of checklists. Instead of simply asking if something might affect your project, they ask how big the effect will be. For example, an assessment questionnaire developed by a Government Agency concerned with IT procurement includes 27 scales on which you can rank your project, grouped under general headings. Under the heading 'Maturity of the Departmental Organisation', one of the scales is between: Clear delegation of authority is practised (score 1); and Centralised management with little delegation (score 4).

If you think your project tends one way or the other without being as extreme as either set of words, you give it a score of 2 or 3.

When all the scores have been assigned they are added together to give a score for the whole project. The theory is that if the score is below a certain threshold you are safe, between the threshold and another limit you stand a chance, and above that limit the risk is very high.

Arbitrary scoring measures like this are useful if they are interpreted realistically. In practice they are either dismissed as meaningless or accorded the status of absolute objective measures, neither of which belief is very useful. They are most valuable, not for the number they produce at the end, but for the way they highlight separate issues and give some indication of which are the most important.

Scoring techniques are a little better than checklists and tables of headings, but not much. It is quite possible for real priorities to be different from those indicated by the scores. This might be because of confusion between a risk's likelihood and its impact, a common problem, or because the score takes no account of your ability to cope with a risk.

Although they appear to give you an aggregate measure of risk, there are two reasons why scoring techniques fall down here too. The relationship between individual risks in a project and the risk to the whole project is more complicated than simple addition, as shown below. The mechanism of assigning scores and adding them up has little to do with risk. On top of this, the fact that any questionnaire limits you to a predefined set of issues means that there will always be a danger of the biggest risk being something new, something novel, something not on the list. Unless your field of operation is very stable and repetitive it is almost certain that every project will have at least one completely new issue to be managed. Because it is new, it will be potentially very risky and the scoring framework will not know about it.

1.2.3 Quantitative techniques

The quantitative techniques to be described in this book start from your existing plans, especially your schedule and costs. They aim to link everything which might go wrong to these structures. Rather than just say that poor definition of the user interface represents a risk (the issue-based assessment), or that it is a moderate risk worth 3 points (the scoring approach), you can say what activities it affects and by how much.

The quantitative assessment approach to this issue could be, for instance, to point out that during user acceptance there is a 1 in 3 chance of the user interface look and feel being rejected.

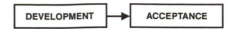

Figure 1.2 Simple sequence of activities

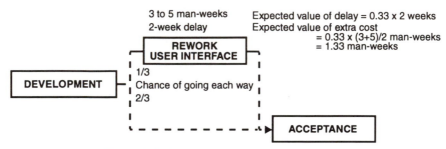

Figure 1.3 Description of uncertainty in plan

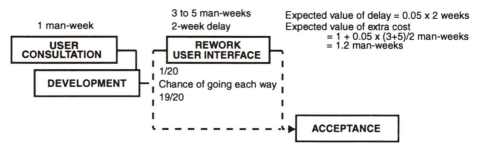

Figure 1.4 Revised plan and uncertainty

Figure 1.2 shows a very simple structure, a development task followed by acceptance. It might be that if the user interface is rejected you can foresee having to spend 3 to 5 man-weeks of effort to put things right, suffering a delay of 2 weeks in the schedule. This is illustrated in Figure 1.3.

You might then find that by allowing for an extra man-week of effort on user consultation early in the project you could reduce the risk of rejection to 1 in 20, or better. This is illustrated in Figure 1.4. The net effect of the uncertainty is described in very simple terms here by the expected or average value of the cost and schedule over-runs.

It is quite likely that you would have been able to sort out this single issue just as well no matter which approach had brought it to your attention. Some will not be so clear-cut, though, and as soon as you have half a dozen significant uncertainties to deal with life gets very difficult.

Quantitative techniques can satisfy all the objectives of risk analysis. Being based on the planning structures you would use anyway, cost breakdowns and schedules, this type of assessment fits in naturally with normal planning and forecasting processes. It uses the same language, the same logical structure and the same measurement units, time and money in most cases. This makes it easy to understand the results of the analysis and easy to interpret them in terms of decisions about your commitments to delivery dates and budgets.

1.3 THE ANALYST

There is no getting away from the fact that quantitative risk assessment requires a certain amount of knowledge and the use of a computer-based tool. You have two choices when you introduce the techniques into your organisation: you can teach everyone concerned to do it themselves, or provide specialist analysts.

Uncertainty and risk are such fundamental features of the way we work and live that it makes a lot of sense for everyone to know the basics. However, for the foreseeable future all sorts of practical problems will prevent this. It will generally be necessary to have at least one person in your organisation take on the role of the specialist, or to have access to an external consultant.

Given that you need one or more specialists, there are (broadly speaking) two models to arrange this. One is to set up a cell of specialists who do all the analysis and advise the rest of the business on risk. The other is to have a small number of consultants, maybe only one, who help others assess and manage the risk. No one can say which approach will best suit your business, but a few general observations can be made.

The risk cell approach puts risk off to one side as a separate topic. There is a danger that project managers may feel that they are responsible for the project and someone else is looking after the risk. It also builds in a split between those who know about the risks, the project team, and those who are expected to discover them, the risk cell. Getting people to admit that things might go wrong is always difficult. Any barrier to openness needs to be considered carefully.

Consultancy support for project managers who take responsibility for risk themselves has the potential to avoid this split. It can be operated so that the project team never feel that anything is being taken away from them. The consultant adds value to what they already know by making it clearer, better-structured and more rigorous. As time goes on this mode of operation has the potential to effect a transfer of skills from the consultant to project teams, extending and strengthening the capability of the organisation as a whole.

There is no absolute divide between the two approaches, and most organisations will adopt a bit of both. On the whole, though, the collaborative consultancy option is more likely to be in tune with other developments in the workplace, such as autonomy and empowerment, than a visibly separate unit looking over project managers' shoulders.

Whichever approach you adopt it pays to give a little thought to the type of people best suited to the task. The immediate technical requirements are not onerous. Anyone who can build spreadsheet models of cost or cash flow can use the techniques in this book. Beyond that it is useful, although by no means essential, for the people leading the way in your organisation to have a little knowledge of statistics and some consultancy skills. Risk is uncomfortable and the analyst needs to be able to get people talking about it without them feeling threatened.

The need for statistical expertise should not be taken too strongly. Statistical concepts are relevant to risk analysis, but undue emphasis on theory can wreck the whole process. The ideal candidate will know enough not to be scared by basic concepts such as expected values and variances, but will not let this get in the way of the real work, the substance of the project and the purpose of the business.

1.4 PAYOFF FROM RISK ANALYSIS

The real world is risky, but conventional approaches to forecasting tend to hide this fact, because they have no place for uncertainty. When we are trying to plan, knowing that we cannot predict the future precisely, the mismatch between our planning methods and the world they are meant to represent creates confusion. We are likely to build in biases and distortions, pad estimates or be unduly optimistic. We need an approach to planning and forecasting which is more in tune with reality, an approach that acknowledges uncertainty from the outset.

Quantitative risk analysis using probabilistic models, allows you to describe the uncertainty you face, in as much or as little detail as you want. It also enables you to aggregate that uncertainty into a view of the total risk faced by your project or business. It has several payoffs for the individuals and the organisations involved.

The first fruit of a risk assessment is a more realistic attitude to the task in hand. By exposing the risks and clarifying the uncertain issues, both the project team, their management and customers can get beyond the confusion which often gives rise to disputes.

When I have assessed the risk to a project schedule as part of an audit of work which was in trouble, it has usually defused the situation. Prior to the assessment, the project team and business management are likely to have been arguing about their two divergent opinions of what could and should be achieved. After the assessment it is fairly clear what will happen, and if that is not satisfactory the work can be replanned on a realistic basis, without unhelpful emotional interjections.

The key to greater realism is better understanding between the parties involved in a project. Risk assessment improves communication between projects, the businesses in which they operate and their customers. It can bring the same benefits within a project, helping to create a common view of the task in hand and the issues to be overcome.

Quantitative risk assessment, as set out in this book, takes an overview of an entire project. It makes no sense to base pricing decisions on an assessment of risks in part of the costs. To commit yourself to a delivery date you need to know about the entire schedule, not just a part of it. The main barriers to reaching a realistic view of the risk to an entire project are complexity and the difficulty of dealing with uncertainty. Look behind any communication breakdown in a project and you are likely to find an area of uncertainty, something which the people involved found too hard or too uncomfortable to resolve.

Risk assessment helps you to overcome complexity and deal realistically with uncertainty by using simple models. Models based on your existing cost breakdown, activity network or business plan allow you to deal with a large problem in manageable pieces. Almost as a side effect of the process, but extremely valuable in its own right, those involved in the plan are forced to express themselves clearly and understand other people's positions. There are fewer unresolved issues in a plan which has been subjected to a risk assessment. This alone means fewer surprises later on.

I think it is true to say that I have yet to take part in a planning exercise where no one has said 'it is too early to plan anything yet, come back in a week when we will have a better idea what is going on', or words to that effect. This attitude is not just lazy, it is dangerous. It leads to decision-making in a vacuum. It is never too early to plan; only the appropriate level of detail changes as your information improves.

At the other end of the spectrum, it is not unusual for people to work themselves, and their staff, to breaking point preparing plans in massive and irrelevant detail. No one bidding for a hundred-thousand-pound contract needs to know if the user manuals will cost £10 or £12 per copy to print when there are only going to be 50 sets produced. This might seem to be an exaggerated example, but it is not unknown for someone to effectively stop work to tie down a cost where the difference will never exceed 0.1% of the contract value.

The way to plan and estimate cost-effectively is to work from the top down, to be able to decide where more detail is needed and where you can call a halt. Since the purpose of planning and estimating is to reduce uncertainty about the future and provide a basis for decision-making, we need to know where the uncertainty is and how to reduce it. Quantitative risk assessment gives you exactly that: measures of uncertainty and insight into its origin.

When a large venture was being considered a few years ago there was a lot of uncertainty about the investment required. Most of the discussion centred around the number of technical staff required for preliminary studies and bid preparation. A risk assessment of the investment phase of the business shifted the emphasis completely.

The risk assessment consisted of drawing up a network of the activities we would have to carry out, describing the uncertainty in the length and staffing of the activities and assessing how that cost would be shared with our consortium partners. The staffing levels were uncertain but we were able to specify maxima and minima for them. The durations of the activities were also uncertain and under the control of the prospective customer, but again we were able to bracket them. Finally, the cost share with our partners was uncertain because we had yet to choose them. Once again we could make intelligent assessments of the ratios we might agree.

The initial response of the sales force was a mixture of 'this is too hard' and 'it's a bit like the last big job we did so it will cost the same'. First estimates of the investment cost and exposure were in the high six-figure range. After the analysis it became clear that the investment could easily be four times greater than first thought. The main surprise was not the size of the investment though. It was the insight into where we faced the greatest uncertainty.

Figure 1.5 shows the proportion of the uncertainty in our total investment due to the three main sources: technical effort, timetable and consortium arrangements. All eyes had been on the number of technical specialists required to tackle this business. The uncertainty in the timetable had at least twice the cost impact, but this was out of our hands. The real killer was the uncertainty about what sort of arrangement we would make with our consortium partners when we chose them.

It might seem obvious with hindsight but in an organisation with a strong technical base the focus tends to be on technical issues. What we were missing until the analysis was carried out was the fact that managerial

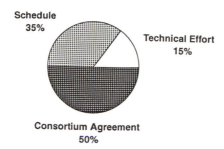

Figure 1.5 Sources of uncertainty in one bid investment

and commercial factors were far more important at this early stage of the programme, and it was these which deserved the greatest attention. The cost-effectiveness of effort spent deciding whether we needed 10 or 15 SSADM analysts in a certain stage of the work, was far lower than that of the effort spent choosing a viable partner and clarifying the cost split with them.

Time is always short, but especially during bids it is invaluable to know where to deploy the half a man-day of free effort you have available to refine your estimates. Quantitative risk assessment makes this apparent.

1.5 OVERVIEW

This book will show you how to carry out quantitative cost and schedule risk analysis of projects. It will also explain how to apply the same methods to forecasting revenue or profit in a projects business.

Each chapter deals with a separate type of analysis, except for Chapter 2 which is an overview of modelling and simulation. It is recommended that all readers take in Chapter 2, as it forms the background for most of the rest of the book. Chapter 3 deals particularly with cost risk. As cost risk analysis is one of the simpler types of assessment, this chapter is also used to introduce some important general concepts. Chapter 3 is also recommended for all readers.

Chapters 4 and 5 deal with schedule risk and business forecasting. With Chapters 2 and 3 under your belt these can be taken in either order. Chapter 6 deals with alternative tools and techniques.

Most of the book is based around a particular modelling tool. It operates within either a Lotus 123 or Excel spreadsheet, retaining the normal spreadsheet user interface. The tool is called *@RISK*, pronounced 'at risk'.

@RISK has been chosen because:

- it provides all the capabilities you need to build cost, schedule, revenue and other risk models;

- it works through a simple spreadsheet user interface which will be familiar to many readers and is easy to learn;

- it costs far less than anything else offering the same functionality.

If you have the time, it is fairly easy to build risk models in BASIC or C++. The object orientation of C++ and the ease with which it can represent mathematical structures make it particularly well suited to building your own risk models, if you know how to use it. With the price of simple tools like *@RISK* amounting to no more than the cost of one or two days professional effort though, most businesses will find it more cost-effective to buy the tool.

2

MODELLING AND SIMULATION

2.1 MODELS

A lot of this book is about models, simple ways to describe the various parts of a plan and how they link together to determine the things you really care about, time and money. Before launching into the detail it is worth saying a bit about modelling in general.

The first thing to get straight is that modelling is not complicated. You almost certainly do it already, so it is not a very big step to move on to risk models. Some people talk about mathematical models as if they must be complicated and can only be used by academics. This has more to do with bolstering academic egos than the reality of modelling. Even accountants build models to represent cash flow, revenue forecasts and similar financial issues, so there cannot be all that much to it!

Simple mathematical models are used in business all the time. They allow us to represent complicated issues in terms of lots of simpler ones. Project planners model their project as a set of linked activities and predict the dates when milestones will be completed, the resource demand of the work and its cost. Business managers use models of future headcount, salary levels, turnover and other factors to plan and manage their operations.

None of these applications of modelling is very difficult to understand, and risk modelling is much the same. You break a complex problem into manageable parts and use a model to describe how they are linked together. The model might be built in a planning tool or a spreadsheet and will consist of a set of simple equations and relationships. Often there is no

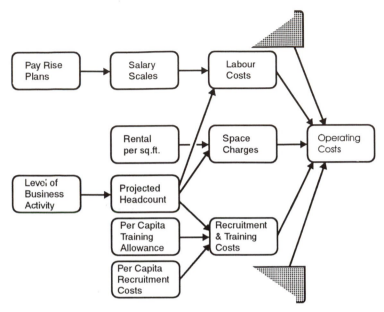

Figure 2.1 A model structure

more to it than a collection of arithmetic: $+$, $-$, $\times$ and $/$. The power of models is not in the complexity of the mathematics, it is in the way the problem is broken down and organised into a structure.

Take a typical example, a financial spreadsheet that represents next year's business plan. It will have several cost and revenue items, phased by month or quarter, and some equations linking these together. Labour costs might be calculated from a projected headcount, salary levels and assumptions about pay rises. Space charges could be based on known rentals per square foot and the headcount. Recruitment and training costs might depend on the level of business activity, the headcount and *per capita* costs of recruitment and training. These are illustrated in Figure 2.1. This structure is the heart of the model, the rest is simple arithmetic: $+$, $-$, $\times$ and $/$.

A risk model will often look much the same as a normal business model. Cost risk models look like standard cost spreadsheets; see Figure 2.2. The only difference is that the risk model includes a little more information, it describes the uncertainty in the costs as well as the values you expect them to have.

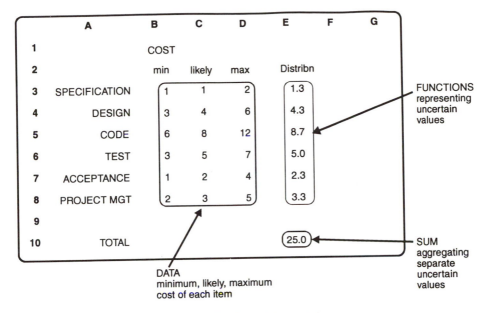

Figure 2.2   Cost risk model

If you can put together a spreadsheet of project costs you can build a project cost risk model. Even if you have not used a spreadsheet before, the process is very simple, and by following the examples in this book you will be able to describe and analyse the uncertainty in your projects or business.

2.2 GETTING THE TOTAL PICTURE

Even a small IT project can easily have tens of cost items to be estimated, and at the time you bid for the work they will all be uncertain to some extent. This uncertainty is absolutely inevitable because we cannot see into the future. The scale of the work required might not be clear, there could be doubt about the complexity of many tasks, and relationships with subcontractors are rarely settled until contracts are awarded. Even when basic issues like this have been sorted out, the speed and cost with which a task can be completed are always hard to predict.

Out of the confused mix of uncertain costs which characterise even simple IT projects, we need a measure of the total cost and the risk it

20 cost items

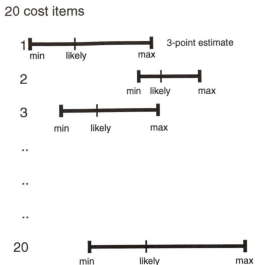

Figure 2.3 Cost model data

entails. If you want to know the cost of something large and complex you break it into parts, define the cost of each part and add them up. If you want to know the duration of a project, you break it into parts, define the duration of each part and the way they are linked together, and then calculate the length of the critical path. The same approach is used to understand the total uncertainty in a project's cost and schedule. We break the project into parts, describe the uncertainty in each part and then work out the uncertainty in the total.

Let us assume that you have a project with 20 cost items. All the costs are uncertain and you need to know how much uncertainty there is in the total cost. The first step is to define the uncertainty in each individual cost; see Figure 2.3. Techniques to describe uncertainty are set out in more detail below. The basic principle is to specify the range that each cost could take, a minimum and a maximum. It is usually possible to specify a most likely value within that range too. The three values together, minimum, likely and maximum, are known as a three-point estimate, a concise description of the possible value of an uncertain cost.

Now you have a description of the 20 uncertain costs, how can you obtain a measure of the overall cost and its uncertainty? One approach would be to add up the minima, add up the likely values and add up the maxima. You might say that these sums represent the minimum, likely and

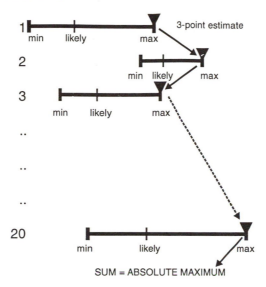

Figure 2.4   Absolute maximum cost

maximum values of the total cost. In principle this is correct, but aside from some mathematical flaws with the likely values it ignores a very important fact about the minima and maxima. The chances of getting anywhere near the extreme minimum and maximum calculated in this way, the best case and worst case, are very small. It is important to understand why this is so.

For the overall cost to reach its absolute maximum, all the component costs must be at their maxima; see Figure 2.4. To obtain some feel for how likely this is to happen, let us assume that you would accept values very close to the maxima as being as good as the maxima; say, values so high that they have only a 1% chance of occurring (see Figure 2.5). What is the chance of all 20 items being in this part of their range? It is 0.01^{20}, 1% multiplied by itself 20 times, or 10^{-40}. This is an extremely small number, so small that you can say that the maximum calculated by adding up all the individual maxima is not a realistic possibility.

Another way of looking at this phenomenon is to say that it is extremely unlikely that 20 independent things will all go wrong at once. If this were not so, projects would be impossible to estimate and plan. Every project manager expects to win on some estimates and lose on others.

So long as the three-point estimates of the component costs are realistic, the extreme minimum and maximum calculated in this simplistic

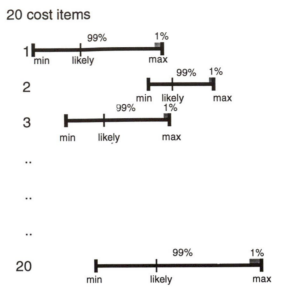

Figure 2.5   Probability of maximum cost arising

way are almost certain not to happen. So how do we assess the realistically likely range of total costs?

2.3 SAMPLING

One way of looking at this problem is that there are lots of possible outcomes. Cost number 1 could be very low, number 2 high, number 3 in the mid-range, number 4 a bit below the likely value, and so on up to the 20th cost. Then again they could all be somewhere else in their ranges. How many combinations are there?

To illustrate the scale of the problem, imagine that you would be content to tie each component cost down to $\pm 5\%$ of its range, so there are 10 characteristic values for each cost; see Figure 2.6. There are 20 costs and 10 values of each one, so there are 10^{20} possible combinations. If you wanted to list them all and you could manage 1 per minute and worked 24 hours a day you could get through about half a million per year. At that rate it would take you about 2×10^{14} years to list all the possible outcomes. If you wanted to tie down costs to better than $\pm 5\%$, or had more than 20

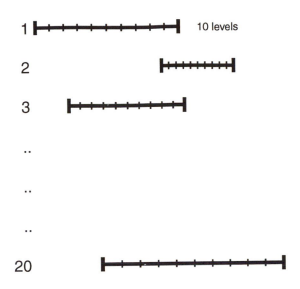

100,000,000,000,000,000,000 possible outcomes

Figure 2.6 Scale of the problem

items, it would take even longer. Listing all the possible outcomes is obviously not practicable.

If traffic engineers want to know the speed of cars on a busy road they do not measure every car's speed. They choose a sample of the cars at random and measure those. If market researchers want to assess reactions to a new toothpaste they do not ask all users of toothpaste what they think, they ask a representative sample. Wherever people study enormous numbers of things, they pick a random sample, measure the items in the sample and extrapolate the findings to the remainder. The same approach is used to assess the likely total cost of a project when there are billions of combinations of component costs which could occur.

Producing a random sample of all the outcomes of a project and using them to assess the entire project is known as Monte Carlo simulation. It is a technique with a long history and a wide range of applications (Kleijnen and van Groenendaal, 1992).

Fuzzy logic methods are gaining acceptance as an alternative mechanism to aggregate uncertain values. Their main application seems to be in situations where the average outcome is the main point of interest,

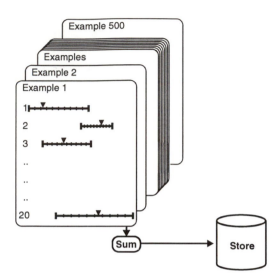

Figure 2.7 Monte Carlo simulation

such as in the control process parameters of household and industrial machinery. Risk assessment is mainly concerned with the spread of values and their relative likelihoods, rather than the central tendency of an uncertain quantity. Monte Carlo simulation provides this wider view of uncertainty and it is so simple that there is little incentive to use anything else.

2.4 MONTE CARLO SIMULATION

A Monte Carlo simulation of the project cost represented in Figure 2.3 would first generate a specific value for each component cost. This would be produced at random but within the constraints of each three-point estimate. These random values would be just one set of the possible component costs which could arise in the project, but they would be realistic. They could really happen.

Next the simulation would calculate the aggregate outcome for the project of these component costs, in this case the total project cost. This value would be stored and then another set of random values would be produced and so on; see Figure 2.7. Typically, 300 to 1000 samples would be produced and their total costs recorded. Less than 300 is usually too few

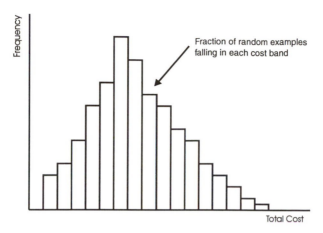

Figure 2.8 Monte Carlo simulation output

to get a representative sample. Once you reach 1000 it makes little difference if you go any further, in most situations.

Each iteration of this cycle generates a realistic possible outcome of the project. It is only one of the possible combinations of the component costs but it could really happen. Each total cost calculated from the randomly generated component costs is an example of the vast number of possible outcomes of the project. The outcomes are generally summarised in a histogram, as illustrated in Figure 2.8.

If the component cost values are generated so that they have the same likelihood of arising in the simulation as in reality, then the total cost they produce will have the same likelihood of arising in the simulation as in reality. This means that if a particular total is exceeded by about 20% of the outcomes of the simulation, it has about a 20% chance of being exceeded in reality; see Figure 2.9.

Histograms have their uses, but in risk assessment we are generally more concerned with the probability of exceeding a target or limit, as in Figure 2.9, than with the probability of falling in a certain narrow band. This is better represented by a cumulative curve, as in Figure 2.10, which shows how many outcomes of the simulation fell above each point between the minimum and maximum recorded. Obviously, 100% fell above the minimum and none above the maximum, by definition.

Quantitative risk assessment does more than help you find the minimum and maximum realistic outcome. It also shows you how the risk falls away in between these extremes. In general the fall off is very

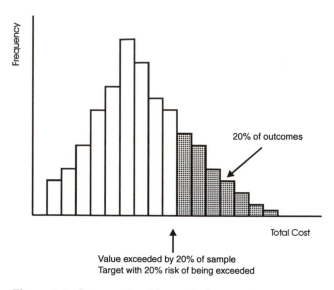

Figure 2.9 Interpreting Monte Carlo simulation output

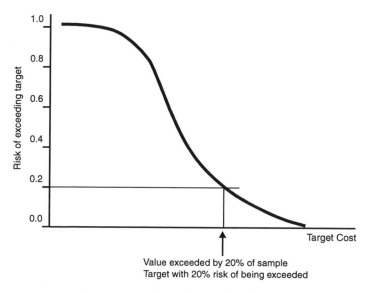

Figure 2.10 Cumulative distribution

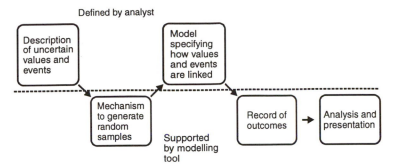

Figure 2.11   Simulation elements

nonlinear. Moving a small way above the minimum only reduces the risk a little; then we enter a region where it falls off quickly, until we near the maximum when it changes slowly again. Most people would want to be working near the right-hand end of such a graph, with a moderate-to-low risk. As well as telling you where the right-hand end is, risk assessment shows you how sensitive the risk is to changes in targets. Yielding a little during negotiation at the far right is not as damaging as in the mid-range. Common sense will tell you this, as well as the simulation, but common sense will not tell you where the far right and the mid-range are.

The example illustrated here is very simple but it has the same structure as any application of Monte Carlo simulation to the assessment of uncertainty; see Figure 2.11. The heart of the process is a model that links detailed characteristics, in this case the component costs, to the overall outcome we are concerned with, in this case the total cost. At the front end are descriptions of the uncertain values of each of the detailed characteristics. The output is a sample of the possible outcomes, reflecting their likelihood of occurring. The mechanics of repeatedly generating random values for the inputs, evaluating the model, storing the results and producing a summary of the output, can be implemented in several ways. The core structure is always the same.

2.5 *@RISK* SIMULATION TOOL

2.5.1 General

@RISK allows you to build Monte Carlo simulations within Lotus 123 and Excel. You retain all the standard spreadsheet capabilities, and on top of these *@RISK* adds three things:

- special functions to specify that some values are uncertain, and to describe that uncertainty

- functionality, that allows you to set up and execute simulations

- a graphical presentation system to display the results of your simulation.

@RISK is not the only software tool you can use to support risk modelling, but at the time of writing it appears to offer the best value for money. A specific modelling system needed to be selected to allow concrete examples to be given, and *@RISK* is the one chosen. There are alternatives, some of which are discussed in Chapter 6.

From here on it is assumed that the reader will be using *@RISK*, either in Lotus 123 Release 2 or Excel 4. The implementation of a model is actually fairly simple once you have decided what you want to achieve, so readers should have little difficulty translating the structures described here to another modelling system. The structures are the heart of the models. The transition from these two versions of *@RISK* to others, such as Lotus 123 Release 3, is very straightforward.

Most of the operation of a simulation is simple and mechanical; it consists of the repeated generation of random numbers, evaluation of the model and the record of the results. This is all handled for you in *@RISK*, once some simple steps have been taken to set a simulation up, defining the number of iterations, etc. All these matters are covered in the *@RISK* manual and will not be repeated here.

Where you will interact closely with *@RISK*, and need to understand what it is doing, is in the special functions used to describe uncertain values. These will be discussed here, as they go to the heart of the way models are constructed.

2.5.2 *@RISK* functions

@RISK adds about 50 new functions to your spreadsheet. The majority of these represent uncertain quantities. They provide you with a way of saying that a value in your spreadsheet is not precisely fixed. It might be a cost which could fall between £10 thousand and £15 thousand, but is most likely to be around £12 thousand. It might be a number of machines required to meet a processing load, which has an 80% chance of being 6 and a 20% chance of being 7.

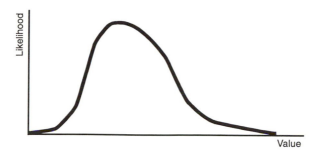

Figure 2.12 Probability density function

If you look in a simple statistics book you will find curves something like that in Figure 2.12. This shows that a certain quantity could fall anywhere in a range, but it is most likely to fall near the value where the curve peaks. The curve is smooth and in principle extends a long way, if not to infinity, in both directions. It is called a probability density function (PDF).

PDFs are a concise way of describing the possible outcomes of an uncertain quantity. In statistics PDFs are used to summarise large numbers of measurements of related values, such as the weights of bags of sugar coming off a production line. They show the range of possible values for the quantity, where it is most likely to fall and how the likelihood of values varies between the minimum and the maximum.

We will be using PDFs in a slightly different way. Instead of making measurements and extracting the range and most likely value from them, we will be specifying the range and most likely value directly. We can then use a PDF to generate a random sample of possible values for the quantity it represents.

2.5.3 Triangular PDFs

For a short while forget about simulations and think how you would describe a single uncertain value, such as an estimated cost. Most estimators would have some feel for the range in which the cost would fall, its minimum and maximum values. Even when information is scarce you can generally make some assessment of the minimum and maximum costs of something. It might be a very wide spread but it can be done. In much the same way, it is not usually too hard to say where in this range the cost is most likely to fall: the most likely value.

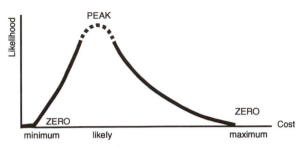

Figure 2.13 Three-point estimate

We now have a three-point estimate of this cost (minimum, likely, maximum). How would we describe the likelihood of values in between the minimum and the maximum? This is not as difficult as you might suspect.

First, the likelihood of any value outside the minimum and maximum is nil, by definition, and so the likelihood must be zero at these extreme points. The next obvious fact is that the most likely value has the highest likelihood, again by definition. This means that the PDF of this cost must start from zero at the minimum, rise to a peak at the most likely value and fall back to zero at the maximum, as shown in Figure 2.13.

Returning now to the simulation, how can we represent a three-point estimate in a model? The obvious answer is by using a PDF. It describes in one place all the values which could arise and how likely they are to happen. Once a PDF has been specified we can calculate the likelihood of any value in the possible range and generate a set of random numbers conforming to that distribution. You can use *@RISK* without knowing how random number generators work.

So the last question standing in the way of a model is, what shape of PDF should we use to represent a three-point estimate? Statisticians will argue for hours about this, but for practical purposes the choice is very simple.

There is a good general principle in modelling: always keep things as simple as you can. We are looking for a PDF shape which will start from zero, rise to a peak and then fall back to zero. The simplest shape which does this is two straight lines or a triangular PDF, as in Figure 2.14. It turns out that this shape is sufficient in the vast majority of practical situations. There is no need to use anything more complex, so hardly anyone does. It has the side benefit of being computationally efficient too, since calculations based on straight line segments are relatively simple.

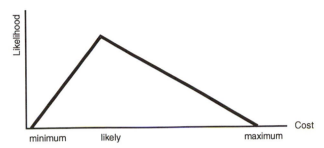

Figure 2.14 Triangular probability density function

We will use triangular PDFs throughout this book. In practice, uniform distributions can also be useful, where you only have a minimum and a maximum to go on, but apart from that most of the other more complex PDFs are not necessary for project risk modelling. A three-point estimate is built into a model with the *@TRIANG* function in Lotus and the *@TRIANG* function in Excel. Each of these has three parameters: the minimum, likely and maximum values of the quantity being represented.

In this book triangular distributions will be defined by their minimum, likely and maximum values. This is usually the easiest way and has the advantage that everyone can understand the relationship between the model and the data used to build it. In the model nothing will ever exceed the maximum or fall below the minimum, and the most likely value is more important than the two extremes. We can use the same words to describe quantities in the model as the estimator might use to talk about the real world. This helps to avoid any mystery creeping into the process.

Occasionally estimators will have difficulty with the absolute nature of the words minimum and maximum. It is not entirely a joke to say that some people have trouble accepting that there is a maximum cost for their task, especially in software development and research environments. If an estimator cannot get to grips with the idea of a maximum you will not get very useful data from him or her. An alternative in these situations is to ask for values which have a 10% chance of being breached in each direction: instead of a minimum, a value which there is 10% chance of being below; instead of a maximum, a value with a 10% chance of being exceeded.

The chance of being below a value which has a 10% chance of being exceeded is 90%; see Figure 2.15. Estimates of this type are, therefore, referred to as 10/90 estimates. There is a 10% chance of being below the lower end and a 90% chance of being below the upper end; the most likely value is used in the same way as before. 10/90 estimates will not be used in

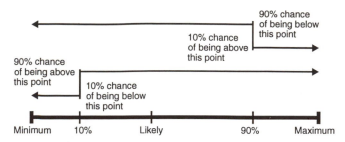

Figure 2.15   10/90 three-point estimates

this book, but they are an important variant on the simpler form. By choosing the *@TRI1090*, *@TRIGEN*, *RiskTri1090* or *RiskTrigen* function in Lotus and Excel, respectively, you can use data supplied in this way just as easily as minimum, likely and maximum values.

2.5.4 Beta distributions

Quite a lot of work on uncertainty in projects has been built around the Beta distribution. This is a smooth curve, rising from zero likelihood to a peak, before falling away again to zero. It can be skewed, so there is a lower chance of falling below the peak than above it or vice versa, by choosing suitable parameters to describe a particular distribution. It has the merit of looking natural, being a smooth curve with a rounded peak, and of being a reasonable approximation to measured data, where measurements are available for multiple examples of more or less identical tasks.

In building risk models we are not seeking a representation of measured data, since there usually is none. We seek to describe our belief about an uncertain value or event with a probability density function which can be used to generate a random sample of values for a simulation. The Beta distribution is not an attractive candidate for this role. It has no extreme values since, like the Normal distribution, it stretches out to infinity in either direction. It also requires some rather obscure parameters to describe it. On both counts it fails the requirement to make models as simple as possible and relate them directly to the data supplied by the estimators in the terms used by the estimators, so the estimators will believe the output of the models. You can use Beta distributions to represent your uncertain values, but none of the models in this book do so.

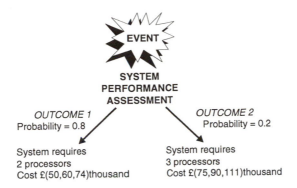

Figure 2.16   Uncertain event

2.5.5 Discrete distributions

A lot of the risk in a project comes from not being able to tie down estimates precisely: uncertain values. This uncertainty is represented in a model with the triangular PDF, as described in the preceding section. There is another type of uncertainty that we need to represent in models: the uncertainty about *what* will happen; that is, uncertain events.

Uncertain events are not as common as uncertain costs or durations but they do arise regularly. Take something as simple as where your project will be sited. Perhaps you plan to house it in your own offices at a well-defined and advantageous rate. However, you know that by the time your project starts other groups might have taken over that space, forcing you to rent offices externally at a higher and less certain rate. On a more technical level you might expect to use two processors to meet a customer's requirement, but know that there is a chance of having to use three.

Uncertain events mean that costs or durations are not just uncertain within a single range; they might fall in one of two ranges (see Figure 2.16). As well as describing the uncertain ranges we need to describe the likelihood of falling in each range. *@RISK* provides a special function to model uncertain events, called *@DISCRETE* in Lotus and *RiskDiscrete* in Excel. The name comes from the fact that the outcome of an event is one of a set of separate or discrete possibilities.

The discrete distribution function is illustrated in Figure 2.17. It allows you to say that the value of a cell in your spreadsheet will be one of two or more separate values. If you wish, these values can be uncertain in their own right, represented by triangular PDFs, as in Figure 2.17.

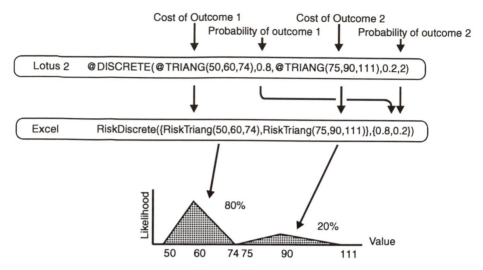

Figure 2.17   Discrete distribution functions

2.5.6 Sources of uncertainty and correlation

Correlation

By specifying three-point estimates you can define the whole range of possible values for each component cost and the likelihood of any value in that range. To complete the picture one more piece of information is required. This is the identity of the source of the uncertainty in each estimate, what it is that will cause it to fall towards the upper or lower end of its range.

We need to know the source of the uncertainty for two reasons. Firstly, it is valuable management information. These sources are the aspects of your project which the current plan does not control. If they were under perfect control there would be no uncertainty, but real plans are never perfect. The three-point estimates show you how far out of control they could get. Knowing the source of the uncertainty is the first step towards understanding how you might control it. The second reason we need this information is to enable us to build realistic models.

If two uncertain quantities are completely unrelated there is a good chance of a high value of one being cancelled out by a low value of another. When a model is being evaluated by Monte Carlo simulation, as described

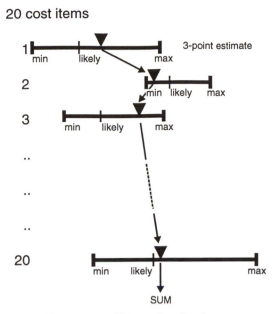

Figure 2.18 Uncorrelated values

earlier, this can happen in the model just as it might in reality. As random values are assigned to the uncertain quantities in the model, some will be set near the top of their range and others near the bottom, as shown in Figure 2.18. This is what we expect to happen in reality too; we win on a few and lose on some others.

When uncertain quantities balance out in this way it helps to reduce the overall uncertainty in the total cost. This is a good thing for project managers, allowing them to pay for over-runs in some areas, with savings from others. Unfortunately it sometimes breaks down. There are situations where two or more quantities are driven by the one underlying source of uncertainty, so if one is high the others will be too, and vice versa. Such quantities are said to be correlated.

Correlated values are all too common and can easily catch you out. For instance, if it takes longer than expected to design a piece of software because the task is more complex than you thought, then it is likely to take longer than expected to code it and to test it; see Figure 2.19. If your system has to record audit trail information and you underestimate its volume, you are likely to underestimate the storage requirements of your system, the network traffic levels and the power required to respond to enquiries at

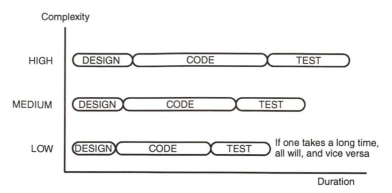

Figure 2.19 Correlation

the required speed. If you overestimate the number of processors you need, you are likely to overestimate the computer room size, its power requirements and air conditioning load.

If there are correlated quantities in your project in real life, you need to represent them in your models. If you fail to do so, the model will be allowing high values of one to be cancelled out by low values of another; in reality they will both be high, both be low or both be in between. The model has to embody the same behaviour as the real world, so its distributions must be correlated too.

Correlation is probably the most commonly overlooked issue in risk management, risk assessment and modelling. Overlooking it in the real world means missing an opportunity to control several parts of your project by getting at the root cause of the uncertainty they face. By leaving it out of models you will make their aggregate behaviour less variable than the real world, because correlation makes extreme values more likely. The reason that very extreme values are unlikely was explained earlier. It is because the chance of lots of things going wrong at the same time is very small. However, if several of those things are driven by a single underlying factor, then only that one thing has to go wrong to generate an extreme outcome.

The effect of correlation is illustrated in Figure 2.20. If some of your project's costs are correlated, then the wider curve will be a realistic representation of the cost risk. If you fail to spot the correlation, or ignore it, then you would calculate the narrower curve. If you use the narrower curve to set targets you are likely to choose one that you think is safe, only

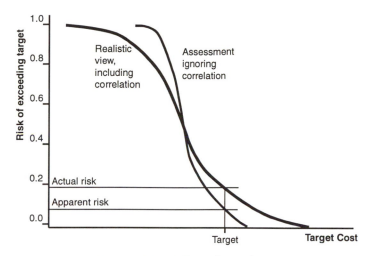

Figure 2.20   Effect of correlation

to find that it is much more difficult to achieve than expected, as in Figure 2.20.

@RISK allows you to link two or more distributions so that they are correlated in your model where you expect the quantities they represent to be correlated in real life. It ensures that if one of a correlated set falls near the bottom of its range then so will the others in that group, if one has a high value they all will; if one is in the middle of its range they all will be, and so on.

The mechanisms *@RISK* uses to link correlated distributions need to take into account the order in which cells in a spreadsheet are evaluated. If there is a group of correlated quantities in your model then at the start of each iteration they could take on any value, so long as each one conforms to its own three-point estimate. The first one in the group can be sampled completely at random. Once that has happened, though, all the others in the group have to follow suit. If the first one happened to be high, all the others must be high, and so on; see Figure 2.21. The first one is independent and all the others depend on it.

You need to decide which distribution in a group is to be independent. It will generally be the first one in the group to be entered as the model is built up, and this is usually the one nearest the top left corner of the spreadsheet. Before going into this and the actual mechanisms for linking correlated values, we need to think about how strongly such quantities are linked.

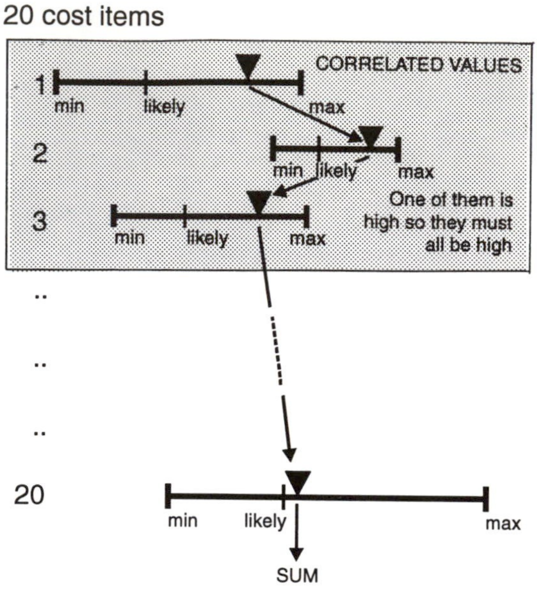

20 cost items

Figure 2.21 Correlated values

Partial correlation

In theory, statistical variables can be completely independent of one another, they can be completely locked together or they can be somewhere in between. These conditions are described as uncorrelated, 100% correlated and partially correlated, respectively.

You might remember from earlier in this chapter that PDFs started life as a way of giving a concise description of an uncertain quantity, summarising a large number of measurements. Risk modelling has turned them around into a method for generating a large number of samples of an uncertain quantity from a concise description. Correlation has much the same place in modelling as PDFs; the concept arose to summarise something and now is used to generate it in a model.

Correlation analysis of experimental data enables you to find out if two or more factors are really linked. If they are there will be a systematic dependence of one on another. When one is high the other will tend to be high and so on. For instance, if you measured the height and weight of a large number of people you would probably find that the two quantities are correlated: tall people tend to weigh more than short people. In the analysis of data, correlation factors are the output, the end of the analysis.

The correlation of weight and height would be high. In modelling we use correlation factors exactly the other way round. We determine in advance that two or more quantities are to be correlated and use a correlation factor to represent this in the model. It is used to control the way the random samples are generated.

@RISK and other modelling tools allow you to represent partial correlations. Partial correlation means that as one quantity rises and falls from one sample to the next in a simulation the other quantity tends to follow, but they are not completely locked together. With partial correlation you can get a high value of one quantity accompanied by a low value of another in the same group. The stronger the correlation the less likely this is to happen, but it is always possible. For instance, the height of people will not be perfectly correlated with their weight. There will be a few tall light people and a few who are short and heavy. The correlation between the lengths and weights of pieces of cable would be much stronger.

Partial correlation can be used in modelling, but most people find it more trouble than it is worth. A model must always make sense to those who have to act on its output, and partial correlation is not an easy concept to grasp. Few people have much difficulty understanding uncorrelated quantities or 100% correlation. These can be explained in simple words and all concerned can see what is happening in the model. Partial correlation is much less transparent and this limits its value.

If you try to use partial correlation two problems arise at once. Firstly, those who are not entirely at home with the inner working of Monte Carlo simulation have difficulty grasping what goes on between partially correlated values during a simulation. It is not as simple as saying that when A takes on a low value so will B, and so on, as you can with 100% correlation. Secondly, while most of us are happy to assign minimum, likely and maximum values to uncertain quantities, estimating meaningful partial correlation levels is less straightforward: is it 40% or 60%, what difference does it make in the model, and what will give a good representation of the real world?

On the whole, when using correlation to represent a link in a project cost or schedule risk model, it is sufficient to say it is either zero or 100%. We are not concerned with statistical analysis, we want to build a model which represents a realistic view of a project, realistic in the sense that we believe it and are prepared to accept, support and act on its findings. In the rest of this book correlation is either not there or it is 100%.

@RISK correlation functions
@RISK provides two ways of linking correlated values, one being

introduced recently as an improvement on that provided with the earlier releases of the package. They only differ if you are using partial correlations, in which case the new one will generally be the most realistic. As we are not concerned with partial correlation it makes no difference which one we choose. The mechanisms look very much the same, they just use different function names. Full details can be found in the *@RISK* manual. In this book the original functions will be used in examples, as they can be used with any release of *@RISK*.

The way you link two or more correlated values is through two special functions called *@INDEP* and *@DEP* in Lotus, and *RiskIndep* and *RiskDep* in Excel. The way they are used might seem a little odd at first, but once you have built a couple of models you will find it straightforward.

Each group of correlated quantities has to be identified, so that *@RISK* knows which values to link together. This is achieved by assigning each group a name, a spreadsheet string. The name is usually chosen to describe the source of the correlation.

The independent member of a group is usually the one in the cell nearest the top left corner of the spreadsheet. It is linked to its group by adding the *@INDEP* or *RiskIndep* function in front of its PDF; see Figure 2.22. The function tells *@RISK* that this value is part of a correlation group and that it is the independent member in that group. The group name is given by the string in brackets after the function name. When the cell containing this function is evaluated, the special function is assigned a value of zero, so it does not affect the value of the cell. However, its presence causes information about the way the PDF is sampled to be recorded and used to control the sampling of all the other quantities in that group.

All other members of the group are linked to the first one by adding the *@DEP* or *RiskDep* function in front of their PDFs; see again Figure 2.22. Once more the special function evaluates to zero, but it causes the following PDF to be sampled in the same way as the independent member of the group. The second argument, shown as a constant with a value of 1 in Figure 2.22, is the degree of correlation. In this book it will always be 1, although it can be anything between -1 and 1, as explained in the *@RISK* manual.

2.6 Summary of Modelling and Simulation

The next three chapters explain how to build models to represent cost, schedule and revenue risk. They require nothing more than the simple

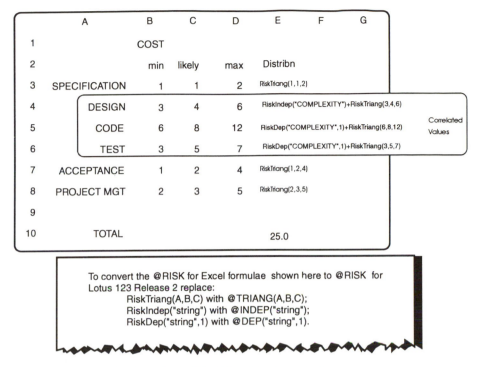

Figure 2.22 Model including correlated values

functions described in the last section and conventional spreadsheet facilities.

The modelling process is much the same for risk as for anything else. You have to break your big problem into parts, define the parts and specify how they go together to make up the whole. Breaking problems into parts and defining how they link together is nothing new, costs are added together and networks of activities have logical connections between them. The only new features of risk modelling are the way we describe uncertain values or events, and the way we evaluate the outcome of the model.

The two basic building blocks of risk models, uncertain values and uncertain events, are fairly simple and have been set out in this chapter. You will find that all the models in this book use no more than these two building blocks, correlations and standard spreadsheet functions.

You can build your own simulations in C++ or BASIC. You can use any programming environment in fact, even spreadsheet macro languages, but it is not usually cost-effective to do so. The @*RISK* package is used in this book to build and evaluate risk models.

Risk models are evaluated by Monte Carlo simulation. This generates a large number of random samples of the possible outcomes of a model, typically several hundred of them. The likelihood of something happening in the simulation is taken to be equivalent to the likelihood of it happening in practice.

Building a model has two major effects. The obvious one is to produce a set of data and information about your project. This is very valuable. You might not realise it at first, but modelling can also have a second effect, tightening up your planning and decision-making processes.

So long as risk remains a woolly and disturbing subject with no clear structure it will be fudged, to the detriment of planning, control and decision-making. Models encourage discipline. It is no longer good enough for anyone to say 'I am worried about X' and abdicate responsibility for the problem. They need to say what the consequences of X will be, in terms of time, money or other concrete measures, and what should be done about it. It might not be possible to estimate the impacts of a risk precisely, but we have a way of modelling imprecise values, using three-point estimates. Imposing the modelling discipline on a planning process greatly improves the realism of plans, and promotes a sense of ownership of the management issues raised by risks. It achieves this by stripping away the mystery from uncertainty, making it just another practical problem to be analysed and managed.

Risk and uncertainty need not be disconcerting. They can be analysed, described, assessed and built into decision-making processes. All you need is a language to use to talk about risk, and a tool to help with the evaluation. The rest of this book explains how you can satisfy these needs cost-effectively.

3

Cost Risk

This chapter explains how to use the basic building blocks outlined in Chapter 2 to model project cost risk, probably the simplest type of project risk modelling. With straightforward projects, where the main risk is due to estimating uncertainty, a first cut analysis can be carried out in an hour or two. If you want to get a feel for risk assessment this is the place to start.

3.1 Uncertainty in Cost Estimates

3.1.1 Overview

Both of the basic building blocks described in Chapter 2, uncertain values and uncertain events, are needed to model project cost risk. Each project will give rise to some uncertain values. Uncertain events with cost impacts do not always arise, but you are bound to come across them eventually, so you need to know how to handle them.

All the estimates which directly or indirectly make up a project's costs will be uncertain. For instance, the complexity and scale of any piece of work will never be tied down exactly in advance, and the efficiency of the team who are to carry out the work is bound to be unpredictable to some extent. Equipment sizing, discounts on hardware purchases, the level of co-operation achieved with subcontractors, and pretty well anything else you can think of, will be uncertain. All of these uncertainties make your estimates of costs uncertain. Most of them will just result in simple uncertain costs, costs you know will be incurred but cannot be sure how large they will be.

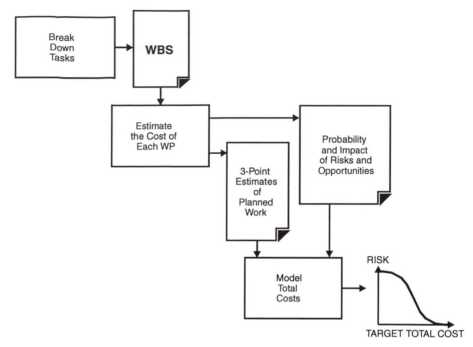

Figure 3.1 Risk assessment process

Some project will also include uncertain events with the potential to add lump sums to the cost. You might plan to obtain equipment from supplier A, but recognise the risk that you could be forced to buy from supplier B at a higher cost if A cannot deliver on time. Your design might be based on five processors, but if the system performance is inadequate you could be forced to pay for a sixth.

To assess the uncertainty in a project's costs we need to break the total cost into parts, describe the uncertainty in each part and then put the parts back together to give a picture of the whole. The standard way to break down a project is by means of a Work Breakdown Structure (WBS) (Turner, 1993). The overall process of project cost risk assessment, starting from a WBS, is illustrated in Figure 3.1.

3.1.2 Using a WBS

A WBS can be drawn up at any level of detail, from a simple top-level view down to the lowest level at which an individual can describe her or his

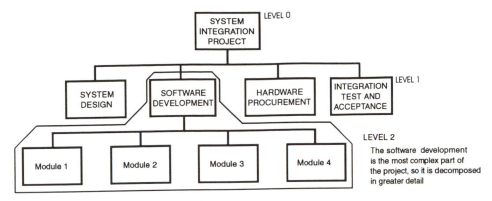

Figure 3.2 Work breakdown structure levels

work. The appropriate level of detail will vary, depending on what you are trying to achieve. Business reports might treat the whole project as a single financial entity. Within the project, control is likely to be exercised in terms of work packages (WPs) two or three levels below the project as a whole. Detailed planning at the working level can be one or two levels lower again.

The appropriate level of detail for a cost risk analysis will depend on several factors. The main one is always the amount of time available to carry out the analysis. In an extreme case you could make a three-point estimate of the entire project's cost, if you have to give a snap response. Given a couple of hours warning, you should have little difficulty going to the next level, where there might be 6 to 10 broad WPs. With a little more time it is usually feasible to get down another level, to a few tens of WPs, and a fairly comprehensive assessment of the cost risk of the project.

The level of decomposition of a WBS need not be uniform. The first level is likely to contain some WPs which are simple and others which are very complex; see Figure 3.2. Not only will the complexity of WPs vary across a WBS, so will the uncertainty in the cost estimates. Hardware purchase costs and software development costs might be of the same order of magnitude, but it is likely that there will be more uncertainty in the software development costs. If you have limited time in which to refine your estimates, which one of these two will you study further? It would obviously be more cost-effective to look into the uncertainty in the software development costs than to examine the hardware purchase prices.

Risk modelling gives you an easy way of deciding where to use scarce estimating effort, always a problem in bidding. No matter how large or

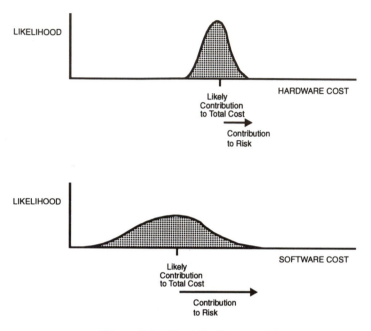

Figure 3.3 Contributions to risk

interesting a cost, if it is relatively well defined it can be put to one side while other costs which represent a greater risk are examined; see Figure 3.3.

3.1.3 Modelling the cost of a single WP

Once a project is broken into WPs we only need to be able to model the WPs one at a time to build a model of the whole project. What is required to build a model of a WP?

The cost of a WP going more or less as planned is represented by a three-point estimate. The uncertainty it describes allows for the fact that you always have limited information about requirements and the rate at which work can be executed. The three-point estimate does not allow for major disruptions, events which effectively require a change of plan. These are represented by discrete events, as shown in Figure 3.4.

Before proceeding it is worth noting that, in spite of what has just been written, three-point estimates are sometimes used to represent major risks.

COMPLETE DESCRIPTION OF A WORKPACKAGE COST

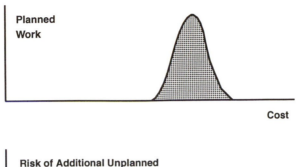

**Planned
Work**

Cost

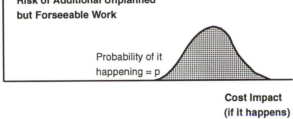

**Risk of Additional Unplanned
but Forseeable Work**

Probability of it
happening = p

**Cost Impact
(if it happens)**

Figure 3.4 Discrete events

This is not recommended, for the following reasons. Suppose, for instance, that you are planning to select a large accounting package and customise it to meet your customer's needs. If your client's business has some unusual features there could be a small risk of finding that none of the available products is suitable and you have to develop a bespoke system. You could set up a three-point estimate with a minimum equal to the cheapest package, the likely value equal to the price of the package you expect to use, and a maximum equal to the maximum cost of the bespoke development; see Figure 3.5.

Using a three-point estimate to represent major risks, as in Figure 3.5, implies that you could be faced with a cost anywhere between the minimum and the maximum. In fact this cost could only fall in either of two ranges, as shown in Figure 3.6. If you can work to your plan, the cost will be uncertain, but it will be confined to the lower range, where the main source of uncertainty is the amount of customising required. If you are forced to switch to a bespoke development the cost will again be uncertain, but within a different and higher range. There is a gap between the two ranges where the cost will never fall. To represent this type of risk with a

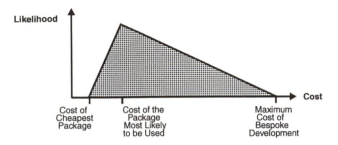

Figure 3.5 Three-point estimate covering an uncertain event

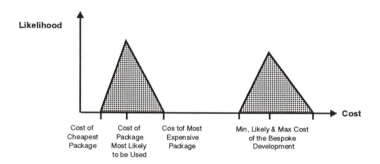

Figure 3.6 Discrete representation of an uncertain event

three-point estimate alone is unrealistic. It is much more meaningful to use a combination of three-point estimates and discrete events. Three-point estimates and discrete distributions are described in Chapter 2.

It is not very common, but there is no reason why one WP should not have its cost influenced by more than one uncertain event. Perhaps the hardware cost is subject to uncertainty about:

- the discount you will negotiate, an uncertain value

- whether you will use three or four processors, an uncertain event

- whether you will buy the processors from supplier A or supplier B, another uncertain event.

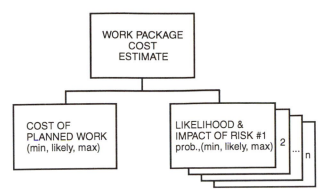

Figure 3.7   Work package cost estimate

So, in general, a WP cost will be represented by an uncertain value, described by a three-point estimate, and a group of uncertain events, described in terms of their likelihood and impact. This is illustrated in Figure 3.7.

An uncertain event is modelled by a discrete distribution, representing the fact that it might happen but it might not, and by a three-point estimate for its impact. It is important to be clear about the way an impact is expressed. It can be expressed as the extra cost if the risk happens or as the total cost if the risk happens, including the base cost, as well as in other ways. Both are equally valid, but if you have the base cost expressed elsewhere it is easier to talk of the impact in terms of the extra cost alone.

3.1.4 Assigning probabilities

Risks which might or might not occur are characterised by their probability or likelihood and their impact. The impact will be an uncertain value and can be modelled with a three-point estimate. This is easy. How do we assign a probability to a risk, though?

You might be used to thinking of probabilities in terms of tossing coins, rolling dice or spinning roulette wheels. It is useful to contrast these familiar concepts with the use of probabilities in risk modelling.

How do you know that a coin has an equal chance of landing heads or tails up, and what do we mean when we make such a statement? Very few of us have sat down and thrown a coin enough times to test the idea that heads and tails are equally likely. If you have an enquiring mind you might have thought about the reasons why a coin would fall one way or the other. Unless you know something I have missed you are likely to have concluded that there is no particular reason for it to fall on one side or the other, neither side is favoured.

Your beliefs about the statistics of coin throwing are probably a mixture of personal experience and what you were told when you were young and impressionable. The same types of information play a role in project estimating and forecasting: what you have seen, direct experience of the same or similar situations in the past; what you have heard, lessons learned from other people; and what you have worked out for yourself, the results of analysis. All of these are used in assigning probabilities to uncertain events.

Imagine that you had nothing better to do for a weekend and you decided to toss a coin several thousand times. Let us assume that you do find the occurrences of heads and tails are near enough equal. The next day someone asks you to bet money on the toss of a coin. Because you know what happened in thousands of similar events you have a good understanding of what will happen on this one, and can decide whether or not to bet and how much to risk. You know how much confidence you have in the coin landing each way up. In this case you are equally confident of both. You believe that a head is as likely as a tail.

When you are faced with an uncertain future event in a project you will hardly ever have been through exactly the same situation before. You will certainly not have been able to try it out hundreds of times to build up a picture of the likelihood of the various possible outcomes. In this situation you have to fall back on experience of similar events, your own experience and that of others, and possibly some analysis of the event. No matter how you arrived at the assessment, it comes back to the same thing as betting on the toss of a coin, your confidence or belief in which one of the possible outcomes will arise.

In Chapter 2 the point was made that PDFs and correlation factors started life as a means of summarising what we see happening in the real world, but risk modelling turns them round into ways of describing our beliefs about the future. Probabilities have gone through the same transition. They started life as a way of summarising the fact that when something was repeated a particular outcome cropped up with a certain frequency. They have been turned around to provide a mechanism for defining how often an event should happen in a Monte Carlo simulation, or how much weight it should have in our decision-making.

If you think a cost is certain to be incurred, you put it directly into the model. Its probability of occurrence is 1, but we do not bother mentioning that. If a cost is not certain to arise its probability of occurrence is less than 1. You need to decide if it is most likely that it will occur or most likely that

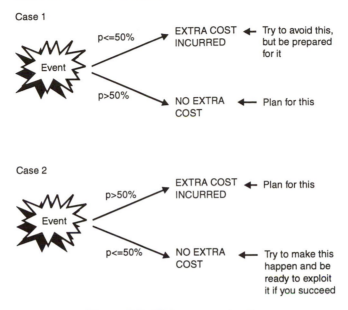

Figure 3.8 Risk or opportunity

it will not; see Figure 3.8. Now you can assign a probability to represent your belief about what will happen.

If you think it is just as likely that the cost will be incurred as it is that it will be avoided, the probability of it happening is 50%. This is the simple case, where there is nothing to choose between the alternatives. If it is not that simple, and one outcome is more likely than the other, you need to put your feelings down as a number, but this is not as difficult as it might at first seem. If we concentrate on the least likely of the two outcomes, whatever that is in any particular case, it has to have a probability less than 50%, and obviously to be meaningful it must be greater than zero.

Unless you have historical information from which to derive probabilities, which is fairly rare in projects and more so in IT projects, attempting too much precision is a mistake. Most people are content to express their probabilities to the nearest 10% (i.e. 10, 20, 30, 40%), or as whole number odds in the same general range (i.e. 1:10, 1:5, 1:4, 1:3). This means that you only need to select from a set of four values, or six if you combine both lists.

3.1.5 Opportunities

It is quite common to find that a plan includes some costs you expect to have to pay, but that there is a chance of getting away with less. For instance you might plan to use existing products in a system, but know that there is a small chance, less than 50%, of a new development being available in time to save you money. It makes sense to put the higher cost in the plan because this is what you expect to happen, but the possible cost saving is a real part of the future you are trying to represent and should be included in the analysis.

There are several ways to deal with this. The easiest one is to treat the possible saving exactly the same as a risk, but to give it a negative impact on the cost. If it does not happen there is no effect, and if it does happen the cost is reduced. It makes more sense to refer to this as an opportunity than a risk, an opportunity to save money. The way it is represented and modelled will be exactly the same as for a risk; the only difference is that the opportunity has a negative impact.

3.2 DATA REQUIREMENTS FOR COST RISK MODELLING

The data requirements for cost risk modelling should be fairly clear from the first part of this chapter, but to make them completely clear they are set out here explicitly. The data structure is based on the Work Breakdown Structure (WBS) made up of Work Packages (WPs).

The first step is to generate a WBS. For each WP in the WBS the following information is then required.

Firstly, a three-point estimate of the cost of the planned work, including everything you expect to happen (probability $\geq$ 50%) and excluding anything you do not expect to happen (probability < 50%). The three-point estimate will consist of the minimum, most likely and maximum values of the cost, with a description of the source of the uncertainty that these three values represent.

Secondly, descriptions of any uncertain events, risks or opportunities which might cause the plan to change. Each description will consist of the probability of the event occurring and a three-point estimate of its impact. There might be no uncertain events affecting a particular WP, there might be one or there could even be several.

This data structure is illustrated in Figure 3.9.

Cost risk data might be backed up with anything from a verbal report to detailed justifications. An example is set out here with a brief description

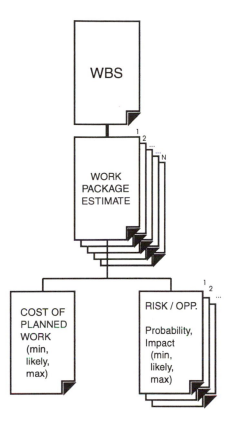

Figure 3.9 Cost risk data

of the basis of the estimates. The data are summarised in Tables 3.1 and 3.2.

3.3 EXAMPLE

This hypothetical but realistic example describes the cost of preparing a bid and the uncertainty in that cost, seen at a high level. It represents the type of analysis which might be carried out for a bid qualification, as part of deciding whether or not to bid. The preparation of a bid for a major project is best treated as a project in its own right.

The activities required to prepare the bid are described in work package (WP) estimates. A brief description of the requirement for which the bid is being offered precedes these estimates, but the estimates refer to the cost of preparing the bid, not the cost of the work if you win the bid.

3.3.1 Requirement description

The bid is for a medium-sized IT system consisting of two Unix processors with 80 intelligent workstations. The software will consist of off-the-shelf applications as well as some customisation and integration. The system is to be installed and the users trained. Part of the bid is for full HW and SW support for 10 years after the system is installed.

All this information has been obtained in discussion with the customer. Specific requirements, especially the identity of the software applications to be bought in, will not be known until the invitation to tender is issued.

The cost of carrying out the implementation is to be evaluated elsewhere and refined during the bid preparation. This example is only concerned with the cost of preparing the bid.

It is expected that the bid will be prepared over a period of eight weeks. The average cost of the bid team staff will be £300 per day.

3.3.2 Work package estimates

Overview

The bid preparation activities have been broken into seven WPs.

100	BID MANAGEMENT
200	SYSTEM DESIGN
300	PURCHASED SOFTWARE
400	SW DEVELOPMENT AND INTEGRATION
500	BUILDING WORKS AND INSTALLATION
600	TRAINING AND INITIAL SUPPORT
700	POST-INSTALLATION SUPPORT

Estimates, with risk analyses, for each of these WPs are set out over the following eight pages:

WP 100, BID MANAGEMENT

Description

This is project management of the bid document production and preparation of the project management sections of the bid. Also, estimating the management costs of the implementation.

Estimate

Expected to require one professional project manager, one planner and one assistant. The assistant may not be full-time, depending on the numbers of WPs in the implementation plan and the number of pages in the proposal.

- Minimum   100 man-days = £30 thousand

- Likely   115 man-days = £34.5 thousand

- Maximum   120 man-days = £36 thousand

Source of uncertainty in this estimate

The number of WP descriptions and pages of proposal text which need to be collated.

Risk assessment for this WP cost

There are no major issues.

WP 200, SYSTEM DESIGN

Description

Specification of the outline system architecture to be offered and the products required to implement it. Describe this architecture in the proposal and estimate the HW costs.

Estimate

This is expected to require one leading designer with between 2½ and 4 effective full-time assistants, depending on how much of your own company's equipment is used. The more the design is based on your own company's equipment, the easier it will be to complete.

There is a chance, assessed at about 20%, that the customer will demand the use of a special access control package. If this happens the bid team will need to hire an external consultant to advise on usage of the access control. In addition, if this package is to be used, one member of the System Design team and one member of the SW Development and Integration team will need to visit the suppliers in the USA for technical and commercial discussions.

- Minimum   140 man-days = £42 thousand
- Likely   180 man-days = £54 thousand
- Maximum   200 man-days = £60 thousand

Source of uncertainty in this estimate

The proportion of the system to be based on your own company's equipment.

Risk assessment for this WP cost

A specialist access control system may be required by the customer. If this happens an external consultant will need to be hired at £500 per day for 2 to 4 weeks, and two people will need to visit the USA at a total cost of between £4 thousand and £7 thousand.

Probability
20%.

Impact

- Minimum   £9 thousand
- Likely   £12 thousand
- Maximum   £17 thousand

Source of uncertainty in impact assessment

Unknown difficulty of designing the interface between the access control system and the operating system.

WP300, PURCHASED SOFTWARE

Description

Identify suppliers, obtain technical specifications and quotes for the bought-in components of the proposed software. Prepare proposal text describing the applications and their place in the system.

Estimate

There are expected to be between three and five bought-in applications, each of which could require about one man-week of effort to investigate and document them for the bid. If a particularly difficult application is chosen it may take two man-weeks, but there is unlikely to be more than one of these.

- Minimum   15 man-days = £4.5 thousand

- Likely   25 man-days = £7.5 thousand

- Maximum   30 man-days = £9 thousand

Source of uncertainty in this estimate

Complexity and number of bought-in applications.

Risk assessment for this WP cost

No major issues.

WP 400, SW DEVELOPMENT AND INTEGRATION

Description

Defines the SW development and integration tasks, describes these in the proposal and estimates their costs.

Estimate

A development manager and a software development team leader are expected to be required to produce this part of the proposal. The level of effort may be less than full-time, depending on the extent to which your own company's products can be used to meet the requirement. There is a chance that a third person may be required to help out. The greater the use of your own company's products, the simpler the task will be.

- Minimum 70 man-days = £21 thousand

- Likely 80 man-days = £24 thousand

- Maximum 100 man-days = £30 thousand

Source of uncertainty in this estimate

The proportion of the system to be based on your own company's products.

Risk assessment for this WP cost

No major issues.

WP 500, BUILDING WORKS AND INSTALLATIONS

Description

Estimate the cost of preparing the building and installing the system, then describe this work in the proposal.

Estimate

This task is expected to require one person about half-time for the duration of the bid.

- Minimum   15 man-days = £4.5 thousand

- Likely   20 man-days = £6 thousand

- Maximum   30 man-days = £9 thousand

Source of uncertainty in this estimate

The complexity of the cabling system will not be known until the system design begins to stabilise and the nature of the building will dictate how much site investigation is required to estimate the cost of the job.

Risk assessment for this WP cost

No major issues.

WP 600, TRAINING AND INITIAL SUPPORT

Description

Assess the type of training required and the cost of developing and delivering it, as well as describing the training approach in the proposal.

Estimate

One training expert is expected to be required about half-time throughout the bid activity. At present the customer is in favour of classroom-based training, but there is a chance, assessed at about 1 in 3, that he may demand CBT backup. This will require additional investigation and planning.

- Minimum   15 man-days = £4.5 thousand

- Likely   20 man-days = £6 thousand

- Maximum   30 man-days = £9 thousand

Source of uncertainty in this estimate

Complexity and number of bought-in applications.

Risk assessment for this WP cost

If the customer demands CBT, additional investigation and planning will be required, probably amounting to an extra person for around three weeks.

Probability

33%.

Impact

- Minimum   12 man-days = £3.6 thousand

- Likely   15 man-days = £4.5 thousand

- Maximum   20 man-days = £6 thousand

Source of uncertainty in impact assessment

Familiarity of the training expert with the bought-in software, for which the CBT will be provided.

WP 700, POST-INSTALLATION SUPPORT

Description

Estimate the annual cost of post installation support and describe how it will be provided.

Estimate

It is expected to require a support specialist full-time for about two weeks near the end of the bid preparation. The more your company's products are used, the easier the task will be.

- Minimum   8 man-days = £2.4 thousand

- Likely   10 man-days = £3 thousand

- Maximum   13 man-days = £3.9 thousand

Source of uncertainty in this estimate

The proportion of the system to be based on your own company's products.

Risk assessment for this WP cost

No major issues.

Summary

Table 3.1 Qualitative summary

WP		Source of uncertainty
100	Bid management	Number of WPs and pages of proposal
200	System design	Proportion of own equipment
RISK	Access control	Interface design complexity
300	Purchased software	Bought-in applications
400	SW development and integration	Proportion of own equipment
500	Building works	Complexity of design and building
600	Training and support	Bought-in applications
RISK	CBT required	Familiarity with bought-in SW
700	Post-installation	Proportion of own equipment

Table 3.2 Quantitative summary

WP		Probability	Estimate (£ thousand)	Correlation
100	Bid management		(30, 34.5, 36)	
200	System design		(42, 54, 60)	CONTENT
RISK	Access control	20%	(9, 12, 17)	
300	Purchased SW		(4.5, 7.5, 9)	COMPLEXITY
400	SW development and integration		(21, 24, 30)	CONTENT
500	Building works		(4.5, 6, 9)	
600	Training support		(4.5, 6, 9)	COMPLEXITY
RISK	CBT required	33%	(3.6, 4.5, 6)	
700	Post-installation		(2.4, 3, 3.9)	CONTENT

3.4 LAYOUT OF MODEL IN SPREADSHEETS

3.4.1 Standard layout

Spreadsheet systems offer the user a great deal of flexibility. This means that there is more than one way to set out a model in a spreadsheet. A particular layout is used in this book. It is not the only one you could use, but it is fairly compact and easy to set up and edit.

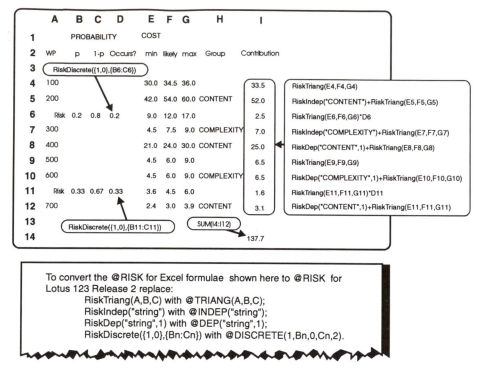

Figure 3.10 Cost risk model

The model layout is illustrated in Figure 3.10 using the data from the preceding section of this chapter. Each WP has at least one line in the model, setting out its basic three-point estimate. Any uncertain events associated with a WP are set out, one to a line, below the basic three-point estimate. The contents of the two types of line, basic estimate and risk, are similar. They are described below.

The basic estimate is specified by its minimum, likely and maximum values in the three columns with those headings. A distribution function is put in the column headed Contribution, to represent the contribution made by this uncertain cost to the total.

Where the estimate is not correlated to anything else, its contribution to the total is represented by a simple triangular distribution. If it is correlated, the special functions described in Chapter 2 must be used to represent this in the model. The member of the correlated group nearest the top of the column is generally taken to be the independent distribution; the other members are dependent on it. For instance, in Figure 3.10, WP 200 is the independent member of the group called CONTENT and WPs 400 and 700 are the dependent members.

The correlation group name is held in the spreadsheet, to clarify the structure of the model, showing which estimates are linked together. In Lotus 123 it is possible to use a cell reference in the *@INDEP* and *@DEP* functions to pick up this group name. In Excel it is necessary to type the name directly into the functions. The benefit of being able to refer to a cell for the correlation group name, as you can in Lotus, is that formulae can be copied from one row to another, limiting the amount of retyping required. The formulae for correlated estimates can be copied from one row to another in Excel, but they need to be edited if the correlation groups are different.

The other columns in the spreadsheet are only used for the risk impact entries, and are blank for a basic estimate.

A risk, or an opportunity, is represented in the model with a similar structure to the basic estimate. It simply has a couple of extra features to simulate the fact that its impact will not necessarily be felt.

The impact of the risk is represented in much the same way as for the basic estimate, its minimum, likely and maximum values are recorded in the appropriate columns. If the impact estimate is correlated with any other estimate this is recorded in the same way as before. The differences are in the columns headed Probability, Occurs? and Contribution.

The probability of the risk arising is entered in the model as a simple number. In the Occurs? column a discrete distribution is placed which will represent whether or not the risk occurs on any one iteration of the simulation. This function takes on the value 1, indicating that the risk has occurred, with the probability in the Probability column. Otherwise it takes on the value 0. This value is used to include or cancel out the contribution of the risk to the total cost.

The entry in the Contribution column consists of two parts multiplied together. One is the same as that for a basic estimate, a triangular distribution with a correlation function where appropriate. In fact, in this example neither of the risk impact estimates is correlated with anything else. The second part of the entry is a reference to the occurrence of the risk. By multiplying the two parts together the risk either has the impact represented by its three-point estimate, or it has no impact at all. If the risk occurs, the impact is multiplied by 1, having no effect on its value. If it does not occur, the impact is multiplied by 0, cancelling it out.

Below all the WP and risk lines is a simple spreadsheet summation function, *@SUM* in Lotus and *SUM* in Excel. This adds all the contributions together on each iteration. It is this value which is recorded as the simulation repeatedly samples the distributions, calculates the contributions and adds them up. If you wish to do so there is nothing to stop

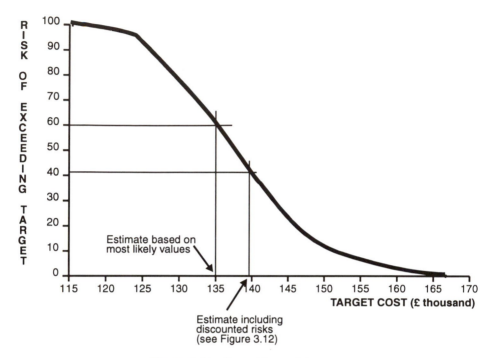

Figure 3.11 Cost risk model output

you setting up subtotals for parts of the cost and having these recorded too. The final steps before you can evaluate the model are:

- defining the output cells in the spreadsheet to be recorded, as the simulation repeatedly samples the distributions and evaluates the totals, subtotals or other values which concern you

- setting the number of iterations to be evaluated, usually between 300 and 1000

- specifying what to do with the results, store them, graph them and so on.

All these points are common to any application of *@RISK* and are well covered in the *@RISK* manual.

The result of running the model is shown in Figure 3.11. It is worth noting that an estimate based on the most likely values of the basic estimates alone has a 60% chance of being exceeded. Even if the risk impacts are added to this estimate, by the conventional method of

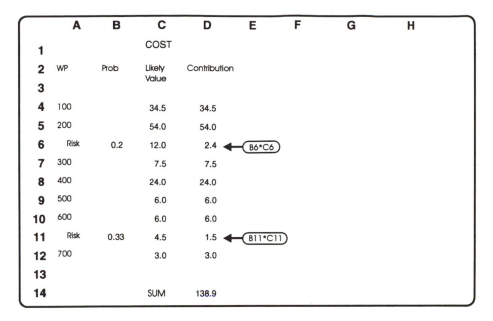

Figure 3.12 Discounted risk impact calculation

multiplying each impact by the probability of it occurring, as shown in Figure 3.12, a simplistic view could lead you to a budget with a risk of over 40%.

3.4.2 Alternative structures

Estimates are sometimes described in proportion to other estimates. For instance, in some types of software development there are accepted ratios between the effort required for design, coding and testing. If some of your estimates are founded on such ratios it is usually easiest to use them directly in the model. For instance, in the fragment of a model in Figure 3.13 only the design contribution is sampled directly. The code and test contributions are calculated from the design contribution, using a simple formula.

Linking estimates through ratios is equivalent to making them correlated. If the first one in the group turns out low, they will all turn out low, and vice versa. The one estimate which is represented by a triangular distribution can still be correlated in the normal way with other distributions of course.

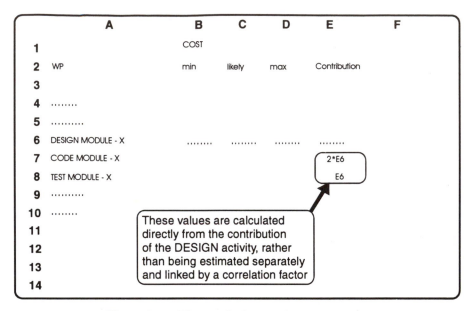

Figure 3.13   Direct calculation of correlated values

If your costs are based on other estimates, such as effort (person-weeks) or quantities of materials, these can be represented directly as three-point estimates in a model. Figure 3.14 shows an example of this where the quantities and the unit costs of a bill of materials are all uncertain. Triangular distributions are used to represent each of the uncertain quantities, and then conventional spreadsheet structures are used to calculate the total cost for each item and add them into the total.

Cost risk models often look a lot like ordinary spreadsheet models. Once you have put the distribution values into the spreadsheet, the rest of the calculations are the same as they would be if you were building a conventional cost spreadsheet.

3.5 HUMAN FACTORS

3.5.1 Risks of risk analysis

Risk is a very personal matter. It is the skills of individual people which give a business the capacity to operate successfully in fields which would be unduly risky for less capable teams. When you start looking into the

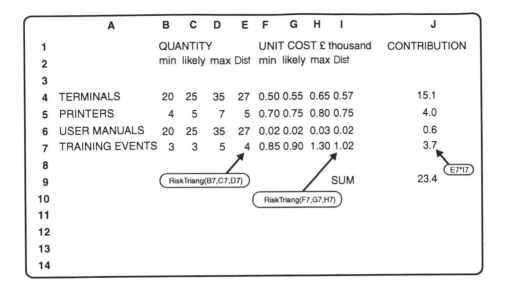

Figure 3.14 Uncertain quantities and unit costs

risks facing a project you are in danger of making these skilled individuals feel that you are questioning their competence.

It is worth being prepared for the negative reactions which can arise during risk analysis before you meet them. Look ahead and prepare your own contingency plans. There are also positive responses you can draw on to help the process run smoothly. It is worth having these at the ready.

As well as the problems of gathering data for your analysis, separate issues arise once the analysis is complete. The stages before and after the number-crunching are discussed in the following two sections.

3.5.2 Data gathering

Objections and responses

There are many excuses for not joining in a risk analysis, but a large proportion can be rephrased as one or more of the following.

- 'Are you saying that I don't know what I am doing?'

- 'It is too early to say anything useful about the estimates, we need more information'.

- 'I know there are risks here but it is my job to handle them, go away'.

The messages you can use to help defuse these objections include the following.

We all have to deal with uncertainty and risk, it is normal and unavoidable. If you are certain that your plans are entirely safe ignore risk analysis, but if there are any problems it can help.

Risk analysis and modelling can help you describe and assess complex risks. This can help you to sort out your own thoughts. It can also help you communicate the issues you face up the hierarchy, supporting internal and external negotiations.

When information is thin, in the early stages of estimating and planning, risk models can give you a realistic view of the ballpark you are working in. You can obtain useful information much earlier than you might expect, and identify where to put effort into reducing the uncertainty.

No matter how clever you are, unless you have been through exactly the same job many many times before, your judgement can be thrown off by complexity and uncertainty. Human intuition gets little training in assessing risk and even a small project, such as the example set out earlier in this chapter, defeats most people. Simple models lighten that load and free your mind to think about how to control the risks.

You might want to draw on the following useful positive responses.

- 'Thank heavens someone has realised there is risk in this work. Now I don't have to cope with it all on my own'.

- 'It is easier to describe the range of things which could happen than try to pretend we can be absolutely precise'.

- 'I am having trouble dealing with this estimating task and the risk modelling approach makes it easier to bottom out'.

- 'I know the real world is uncertain and it makes more sense to work this way'.

With experience you will be able to put the case for using these techniques well enough to soften, if not entirely eliminate, the objections before they arise.

Subjectivity

A general objection which cuts across the whole process is that the information going into the model is subjective. The implication is that the output of the model is, therefore, of no use. To counter this you only have to ask for an example of a plan or estimate which does not rely on human judgement somewhere. Even systems based on historical data pass by a human for checking and interpretation before the results are used.

Human estimators will always be drawing on past experience, their own and that of other people, and adjusting it to allow for the special factors of the case they are now looking at. No estimate is untouched by human hand. Even historical data have to be cleaned up and adjusted before anyone can use them.

It comes as a shock to some people to realise that there is no such thing as a really objective estimate. In fact the very concept makes no sense. Risk modelling is no different from standard planning and forecasting in this respect. It is just a more realistic and effective way of dealing with the subjectivity we are bound to face.

Selling risk analysis

Most people who learn about risk modelling appear to feel it is a good idea. Because you are still reading, you have probably come to the same conclusion yourself. It is easy to forget that the people you need to work with, assuming that you are not estimating and planning in isolation, have yet to see the light.

Before embarking on any particular exercise it is worth setting out what you will be doing and why. A short introduction to the topic can be built around the following points.

- We all know that estimates cannot be absolutely precise.

- I want to find out how much uncertainty there is in each major work package, describe it with three-point estimates, and understand the source of the uncertainty.

- We can use that information to calculate the uncertainty in the total cost, so we can determine what will be a realistic budget.

You can leave issues like describing major risks and uncertain events until you get started and they begin to crop up. Once you get people working with three-point estimates, it is easy to extend the idea.

Contrary to expectations, it is rarely necessary to explain the modelling process or how Monte Carlo simulation works. Most people are surprisingly happy to accept it at face value. This has a lot to do with the results making sense. If they do not make sense your model is either flawed or telling you something you had not spotted. Either way, you need to explore the discrepancy between expectations and results: one of them has to change.

It is generally accepted that you have little chance of getting risk assessment accepted without high-level support. If you intend to use these methods just to ensure that your commitments to the rest of your organisation are safe, or if you are at the top of your particular tree, this is not a problem. Otherwise you need the support of those above you who are to use the information you produce. Backing to help you win this support generally comes from even more senior management or from customers.

Some customers, especially government bodies, are gradually coming to insist on risk assessments in bids. They want to see that the commitments being made to them are realistic. They also use risk analysis as an indicator of a supplier's competence in planning. You are unlikely to expose your cost risk assessment to a customer, but schedule assessments, covered in the next chapter, are a powerful sales tool. Once the use of risk modelling for the schedule has been accepted it is a very small step to using it internally on costs.

By far the most productive means of getting risk assessment off the ground is to have senior management demanding it. The output of a risk assessment is particularly useful for management decision-making. It exposes the risks which are the major preoccupation of anyone managing a project business, and provides a sound basis for setting budgets and targets. Many business managers take to the cumulative distribution immediately. It reflects the way they see a world which they know is uncertain.

If you need a hook to get your management interested in risk assessment, it is worth considering its value as a sales aid. As was mentioned above, this is more relevant to schedule analysis than cost analysis. A schedule risk assessment gives a customer confidence that what he is buying will be delivered. Confidence is valuable and makes your proposal look more attractive. Risk assessment helps you to build that confidence.

Using the results

After you have a model which you and the others involved can believe, what do you do next? This is a human issue, not a question of mathematical modelling.

The output of a cost risk model tells you the range of realistically likely costs you could face. It also gives you a measure of the risk you face, depending on the target you set. Now you have three decisions to make, three limits to set:

- a price

- a project budget, including contingency

- and a target cost, excluding contingency.

The most important limit is the price. This will often be dictated by external factors such as customer expectations or the competition. You would generally want to be sure there was little or no risk of the costs exceeding the price. It might be that on the first pass of planning your estimates are too close to the guide price, or even exceed it. This often leads to confusion, but in fact your options are clear. You have three choices:

- replan the work, finding a cheaper way to do it

- accept the risk, usually for strategic reasons, perhaps offsetting the potential loss against other profit-making business

- decline to bid.

The second limit is the project budget, the cost limit for the project. Exceeding the budget is not quite as serious as exceeding the price. It erodes the margin but does not necessarily mean making a loss. The margin is important though. It represents the return your shareholders get on their capital. It is usually possible to set a price which represents little or no risk of making a loss. It is less common to be able to set a budget high enough to be sure that the margin is absolutely safe. Many analysts and managers work on budgets at about the 20% risk level. As explained earlier in this book, this is more a measure of difficulty than a statistical risk. Targets with a 20% risk seem to be achievable, if not an easy ride.

The third limit is the project's target cost, the part of the budget released by the business to the project team. The part retained by the business is the project contingency. Exactly how the contingency is managed is a local business decision. The principle of retaining a contingency between the commitment made at the business level, the budget, and the target for the project is sound risk management. It reduces the chance of eroding the margin, so long as a realistic risk assessment has been made in the first place.

Contingencies are often thought of in terms of percentages of the total estimate and nice round numbers, 5, 10, 15 and 20% being the most common. Only with a quantitative risk assessment can you arrive at realistic contingencies. The effect on risk of adding a 10% contingency in one case might be negligible on an easy job, and severe on a risky job; see Figure 3.15. In one case you would be handing the project an easy ride, and in the other they could be in trouble before they start. Neither strategy will do much for the team's motivation. Cost-effective performance depends on enough risk to provide a spur, with enough confidence to make people believe they can win.

3.5.3 Risk and 'normal' estimates

Risk assessment will often be carried out alongside conventional estimating and planning. This is particularly common where risk analysis is being first introduced. In the long term it makes more sense to use risk modelling techniques as the core of your estimating processes. They deal with the world as it really is, uncertain and risky. However, it is unrealistic to expect people to change overnight.

When you start you are likely to have a cumulative distribution of costs from the risk analysis, and a single number from the conventional planning; see Figure 3.16. You need to bring the two together. The easiest way is to call the single value 'the estimate', and refer to your work as a risk analysis of 'the estimate'. If you conclude that the estimate has a high risk of being exceeded, it just means that the project is risky, not that the estimators got it wrong.

The simplest and most common way forward is to choose a project budget, usually at around 20% risk, and set a contingency equal to the gap

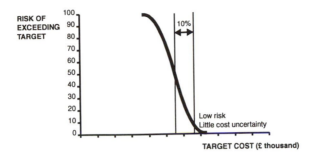

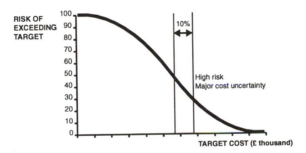

Figure 3.15 Contingencies

between this and the estimate; see Figure 3.17. Occasionally you might find that the estimate is so low that it is unrealistic; then a complete revision of the estimates might be necessary. Alternatively, you might find that the estimators have been unduly pessimistic and the estimate can be reduced, but this is very rare.

If you settle on a project target that is different from the estimate, you need to delegate this to each of the top-level WPs. You can use risk modelling concepts to break the total budget down, so that everyone faces the same risk, being fair to all concerned. However, it is usually acceptable on small- to medium-sized projects to scale everything linearly. So if, for instance, the estimate is to be increased by 15% at the top level to make it realistically achievable, the simplest way of accommodating this is to increase all WP budgets by 15%. This might leave some with a tougher target than others, but as a first cut, with the use of a bit of common sense judgement, it is likely to be adequate. Risk modelling is not a straight-

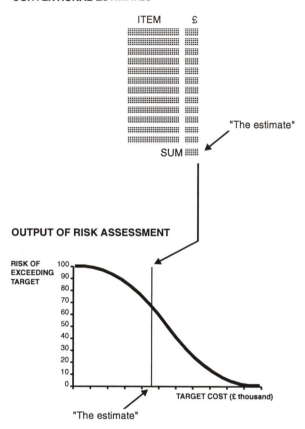

Figure 3.16 Links to standard estimates

jacket. It is simply a support tool, helping you to make decisions but not making them for you.

3.6 Cost Risk Prompt List

Experience and common sense will alert you to most of the risks and sources of estimating uncertainty in a project. However, when you are just getting to grips with a job, or it is a bit different from your normal work, or you want to double-check your plans, then a list of standard risks can be

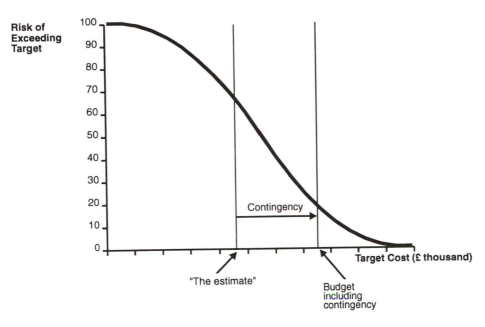

Figure 3.17 Contingency setting

useful. The prompt list set out below will help you to think through some of the common risks that affect IT projects.

It is very important to realise that this is not a checklist. The idea behind a checklist is that if you have covered everything on the list you are safe. There will never be a complete checklist of risks. The world is changing, and anyone preparing estimates has to be ready to think creatively about what could happen and how to respond to it. You can never be sure you have thought of everything. You can maximise your chances by using prompt lists, keeping an open mind and consulting as widely as possible, but you cannot afford to be complacent.

Prompt lists can be anything from a disconnected set of points to a structured tree of questions and answers. The lists in this book are organised under a few headings. For cost risk the headings are very simple, based on the old standby what, who, how and when. This is easy to remember and will generally lead you through the main issues that affect a WP.

It can be useful to build up a list of the standard issues which have afflicted your projects in the past. These will be specific to your particular area of business. Always remember, though, that neither the lists in this book nor your own prompt lists can cover everything which might go wrong. You always need to stop and think, 'what else could happen?'

3.6.1 What

Definition: Is the work content defined in detail, or might you have to carry out tasks for which there is no budget? Could the work content be changed, as opposed to simply extended, in such a way as to increase your costs without increasing your revenue? Is the scale of the task clear, or could it be significantly greater than that for which you have estimated? Are all the assumptions which limit the scale and define the content of the project clearly stated and contractually binding, or are you carrying the risk on any of them? The standard mechanism to remove issues of this sort is a clear definition of deliverables, complete with dates, standards and so on in the proposal. However, it is not always commercially acceptable to make a proposal appear too legalistic, and there are sometimes real uncertainties that the customer wants to pass to the contractor.

Familiarity: Is the content of the project something with which you are familiar? Is your customer familiar with procurement of this type, or could he have unrealistic expectations of what will be delivered?

Maturity: Is the technical content mature or still evolving? Are any of the components still in development? Are any of the components nearing the end of their life cycle, and in danger of becoming unsupported or even unavailable before the contract is completed?

3.6.2 Who

Personnel: Are the personnel on which cost estimates have been based definitely available at the time required, or could you be forced to hire contractors at a premium? Are the work rates assumed to be consistent with the staff who will actually carry out the work, as opposed to that which could be achieved by the expert who prepared the estimates? Does the professional effort profile take into account the time delay, cost and diversion of effort required to recruit staff and bring them up to speed? Where you are using subcontractors all these questions apply equally well to them and their staff. They might be on fixed price contracts, but if things start to go wrong they are likely to try to pass extra costs on to you.

Companies: If you are working in a partnership, a consortium or some other teaming arrangement, is the separation of responsibilities clear or could you find your company bearing costs that you thought would be carried by your partners? Can you be sure that the sum of your subcontractors' commitments fully meets your requirements, or are there grey areas where you might have to commission additional work to complete the contract? Inter-company issues often become difficult when requirements definition, design and implementation are carried out by separate companies. It is usually the prime contractor who bears the pain, at least in the short term.

3.6.3 How

Methods: Is it clear which standards you must work to and are the customer's expectations the same as yours? Are the staff you intend to use familiar with the methods you expect them to operate?

Operations: Are the commercial arrangements standard for your company? Are any internal arrangements, such as resources being made available from another section or division, underwritten at a high enough level to be sure you will not need to buy external resources or other services? Is the scale of the task markedly greater or smaller than what you are used to? Is the duration of the project markedly greater or smaller than what you are used to? Is the infrastructure of facilities, resource management, space, communications, etc., certain to be in place, as assumed in the estimates? In the IT business there is a predisposition to focus on technical issues, leaving operational problems until it is too late to avoid them having an impact.

3.6.4 When

Resources: Have you allowed for the possibility of effort rates, support costs and other charges to rise from year to year? Are the demands of your project for effort, space and other resources reconciled with those of other projects in the same business? Have you considered the chance of key inputs, such as products or access to facilities, being late?

Cash flow: Have you allowed for the cost of borrowing to cover the cash flow? Do any payments fall at about the time your customer might want to save cash by holding up payments, such as just before a financial or calendar year end?

4

SCHEDULE RISK

4.1 UNCERTAINTY IN PROJECT SCHEDULES

Schedule uncertainty is derived from much the same issues as cost uncertainty. When labour is in fact the main cost in an activity, cost and schedule uncertainty are usually the same, being linked through the labour rate. The main difference between the analysis of cost and schedule risk is that a schedule is represented in terms of a network of linked activities, a more complex structure than a list of costs to be added up.

Conventional schedule planning is based on activity networks which are analysed to find the critical or longest possible path from start to finish. Schedule risk analysis operates in much the same way, but allows for uncertainty in the definition of the network, its durations and its logical structure.

The linkages between activities can be complicated but, as with cost modelling, a few simple components are enough to cover the vast majority of real-life situations. The usual links between activities are all used in schedule risk models: FS, finish to start; SS, start to start; FF, finish to finish; as illustrated in Figure 4.1. Lags can be attached to any of these links to represent delays between events in one activity and those in its successor.

One type of linkage used in schedule risk models is not common in conventional project planning networks. Where the course of a project might take one of two or more distinct paths, this is represented in a schedule risk model by a feature known as a branching point; see Figure 4.2. This is a point where you cannot be sure exactly what will happen,

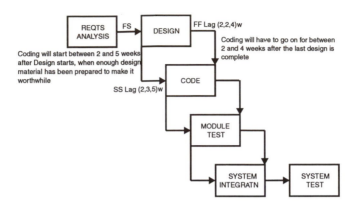

Figure 4.1 Schedule cost model links

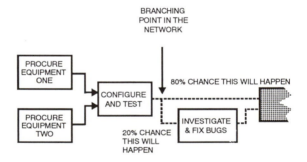

Figure 4.2 Network branching

such as the conclusion of trials which could succeed or fail. The most likely branch will be the main plan and the least likely branch the contingency plan.

Standard planning tools do not allow the representation of contingency activities, even though they can be very important. Being out of sight they tend to slip out of mind and even those who should know better are surprised when it becomes necessary to switch to *'plan B'*. Schedule risk models can incorporate contingency plans in a realistic way, ensuring that they are taken into account and remain in view.

The basic form of a schedule risk model is: a network, with all the dependencies between activities; three-point estimates for the durations of all activities, including contingencies, and lags on links; definitions of correlations between estimates; and the probabilities associated with branching points.

More complex structures can be constructed, but this set of building blocks will meet the vast majority of modelling requirements.

4.2 SCHEDULE RISK MODELLING PROCESS

4.2.1 The network

The first step in creating a schedule risk model is to create an activity network. If you already have a project network to hand it can be the basis of your model. If the network has yet to be prepared, the one used for risk modelling will usually be a very good basis for the conventional plan which will be developed later.

Standard planning tools are often used to sketch out the skeleton of a risk model. They cannot represent the contingency plans but, if you have few or none of these, a standard tool is a convenient way of recording the logical links between activities. When you have no branching points at all, a standard planning tool is a good way of producing a picture of your network. If branching does play a role, it might be necessary to draw the model manually, using a graphical presentation package to achieve publication quality if this is required. In many cases pencil and paper are all that is needed.

The purpose of the picture of a risk model's network is two-fold. You will eventually use it to build the actual model in *@RISK*. However, while you are building up the model, a picture of the network is by far the best basis for a discussion of the relationship between activities and the estimates associated with them. For these purposes production-quality drawings are not necessary. Something like the sketch shown in Figure 4.3 is more appropriate. Large sheets of paper, a pencil and eraser are the best tools.

Scale of network

The number of activities in a schedule risk model needs to be chosen to strike a balance between competing requirements. The more activities you use the easier it will be to show the detailed relationship between different parts of the project. However, if the network becomes too large it can

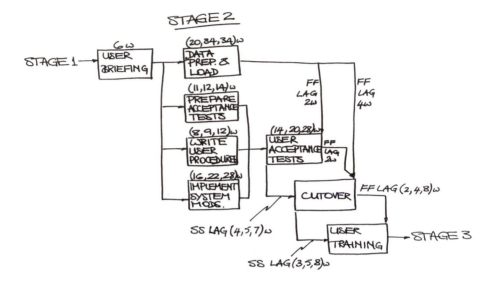

Figure 4.3 Working drawing of a network

become unintelligible, and the work required to model it in a simulation grows out of proportion to the number of activities.

A good general rule is that any model should be able to be described in a single drawing. If extra detail is necessary, it can be accommodated in a hierarchy of models, with some parts of the top level structure being expanded into sub-models; see Figure 4.4. Models of a few tens of activities, between 10 and 100, tend to prove both manageable and comprehensible. You can use more, but the model is likely to become unwieldy, and no one can really grasp all the issues in a structure with 200 interlinked elements if it is not summarised in some way. Editing and validating large models, especially while this remains a manual task, is also much more error-prone than for smaller models. An example of a typical schedule risk model is shown in Figure 4.5.

Building the network

If you already have a network for your project on a conventional planning system, it can be used as the starting point for your risk model. More commonly, in the early stages of planning and during bids, the risk model comes before anyone has got around to planning in earnest. Either way

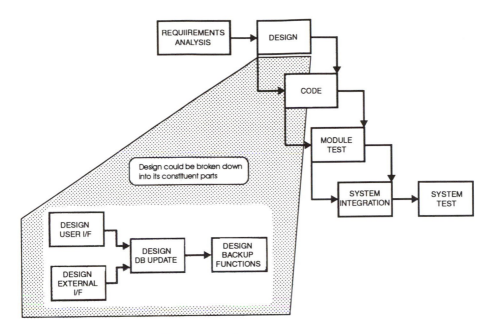

Figure 4.4 Hierarchy of models

there will be some differences between the network you use for risk modelling and the one you use for controlling a project.

A schedule risk model only needs to contain those activities with a direct bearing on the dates you are concerned with, major milestones and the end. All the hammock activities, such as QA, project management, configuration management and so on, can be left out of a schedule risk model. They need to be incorporated in the costs but they are rarely an important influence on the completion date.

A control plan is likely to show detail where it is necessary to reflect the structure of the deliverables and the separation of work between parts of the project organisation. A risk model requires detail where there are major uncertainties or complex dependencies between activities. The two types of network must be consistent with one another, but they will often differ in detail.

When building a schedule risk model network, a balance has to be struck between: having enough detail to allow a realistic description of the uncertainty and interdependence in each part of the project schedule; and containing the scale of the model and the analysis to a level which is

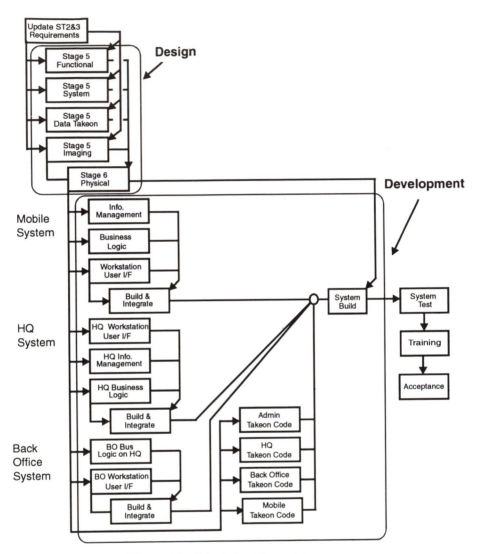

Figure 4.5 Schedule risk model structure

manageable in a reasonable time, and that is within the grasp of the decision-makers who will use the output of the model.

The only way to get a feel for what works is to try it.

4.2.2 Collecting estimates

A schedule risk model can be built up entirely independently of a cost risk model for the same project. However, especially where the main cost is labour, the two are usually closely related. An underlying assumption of many plans is that tasks will be carried out by teams of a fixed size, which means that to a first approximation the cost and duration of a task are proportional to one another: if the task takes 10% longer it costs 10% more. In such cases the cost estimates, which might well have been produced earlier, are a good basis for the initial schedule estimates. If the cost of a task could go up by 25% and down by 10% from its most likely value, then so could the duration.

Simple relationships between cost and duration do not always hold. It is important to look at each estimate carefully and decide if you believe the three values. External events might constrain an activity, for instance. Occasionally, a flexible resource pool might mean that the level of effort can be raised to avoid a potential over-run, so the cost might go up but the duration will not. A design study might be curtailed if there is a danger of an over-run, putting a ceiling on both the cost and the duration.

In many cases the schedule estimates need to be derived from scratch. This is very much the same as cost estimating. A duration is represented by a three-point estimate, with a note being made of the source of the uncertainty. Where there are uncertain events which would change the course of the project, they must be defined as they are for uncertain events with a cost impact, by specifying the likelihood of each one and the sequence of activities to which it it would lead, its outcome. All activities in a contingency plan must be specified, in exactly the same way as activities in the main plan.

4.3 SCHEDULE RISK MODELS

Once you have described the uncertainty in the parts of your project schedule, you need to get it into a Monte Carlo simulation framework to evaluate the project as a whole. A spreadsheet is not the most obvious tool in which to represent a network, but *@RISK* is the simplest way to get the Monte Carlo simulation facilities you need. All it takes to bring the two together is a structure to represent network dependencies in a spreadsheet.

To represent a network we need activities with a start, duration and end for each one. A simple tabular layout, with a row per activity and a column each for the start, duration and end, provides places for all the

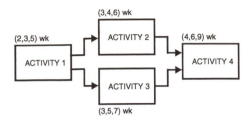

Figure 4.6 Simple network

necessary variables. Figures 4.6—4.9 show examples of simple networks represented in this way.

4.3.1 Finish — start links

Figure 4.6 shows a network which contains only Finish — Start (FS) links. The network logic is very simple. When activity 1 ends, activities 2 and 3 start. When both of these end, activity 4 starts. The durations of all the activities are uncertain and are represented by three-point estimates.

Figure 4.7 shows the network in Figure 4.6 as a spreadsheet model. The end of each activity is calculated by adding its start and duration together, as you would expect. The dependency of activities 2 and 3 on activity 1 is implemented with a simple formula, making their start values equal to the end of activity 1. When the simulation is under way, the duration of activity 1 will vary from one iteration to the next. This will be reflected in the end of activity 1 and so in the starts of activities 2 and 3.

The start of activity 4 is a little more complex, but not much. Activity 4 can only start when both its predecessors have been completed. The standard spreadsheet function *@MAX* or *MAX* implements this dependency by making the start of activity 4 equal to the largest end value of its predecessors. Which one takes longest will dictate the start of activity 4.

When this model is evaluated the end of activity 4 is specified as the output. It is the end of the network. With the start of activity 1 set to zero, the end of activity 4 is in fact the duration of the whole network. When the simulation runs, the activities' durations are sampled, the formulae are evaluated to calculate the end of the network, and that value is recorded.

If your network is built entirely of FS links you need no more than this to build a network of any size you wish. In practice, FS links are rarely

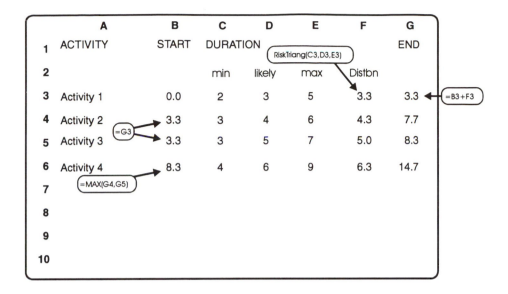

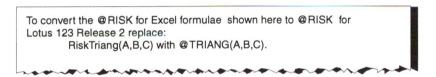

Figure 4.7 Model of simple network

sufficient. The high-level view taken for risk models almost always leads to some Start−Start (SS) and Finish−Finish (FF) links being used.

4.3.2 Start−start, finish−finish links and lags

A typical software system development project outline is shown in Figure 4.1. If it was expanded into more detail there would be clear FS links between the design, code, test and so on of each individual module of code. At the top level all we can say is that coding will start when a certain amount of design work is complete, and it will continue for a specified period after the last design has been delivered. Both the activity durations and the lags on the SS and FF links are uncertain.

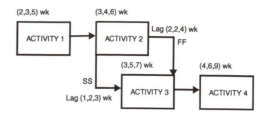

Figure 4.8 Network with lags

Lags can be written in directly to the equations for activities' starts and ends, but this makes the equations complicated and obscure. It is a lot easier to build and edit your model if you represent lags explicitly, in much the same way as activities. They are after all entities with a start, duration and end.

Figure 4.8 shows a simple model network with SS and FF links, with lags as well as some FS links. Each activity and lag is described on a separate line, with a start, an uncertain duration and an end. Figure 4.9 shows this built into a spreadsheet model, with triangular distributions for the uncertain durations.

Apart from the fact that there are two things in the model with durations, activities and lags, the use of functions to represent the network logic is much the same as before. The only significant difference is the use of the *@MAX* or *MAX* function to define the end of activity 3. This activity's end could be dictated by the end of activity 2 and the lag on the FF link. Alternatively, it could be dictated by the time taken to carry out activity 3 itself.

If activity 2 was a design task and activity 3 coding, this logic represents the fact that coding must go on for a certain amount of time after design ends, but it is also resource-constrained. This means that if design ends early, the work of coding will need to carry on for a minimum amount of time anyway. Correlation between the durations of the two activities is ignored here for simplicity but could easily be incorporated into the same structure by adding the correlation functions to the durations of the activities.

Sometimes an activity with SS and FF dependencies is passive, in the sense that it is strictly determined by its predecessor. If this was the case activity 3 would have no duration function; its duration would be calculated by subtracting its start from its end. It could even be left out of the model as it plays no part in determining the duration of the network; this is illustrated in Figure 4.10.

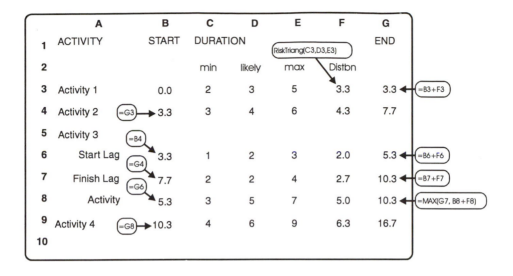

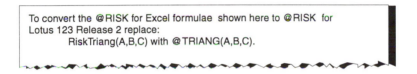

Figure 4.9 Model of network with lags

4.3.3 Probabilistic branching

The structures that you can build with FS, SS and FF links between activities are familiar to anyone who has used a conventional project planning tool. One of the main weaknesses of these tools for estimating, as opposed to the monitoring and control which come later, is their inability to represent contingency activities. There is no way to show that at a certain point in the project you expect one thing to happen but need to be prepared for another. Such points are known as branching points, points where the actual work could follow one of two or more routes through the activity network.

Figure 4.11 shows an example of network branching. This is something which affects almost every task at some level. There are always choices to be made about how to do the next part of the job, depending on how the last part turned out. However, in many projects these decisions only arise at the detailed working level and do not concern issues big enough to be

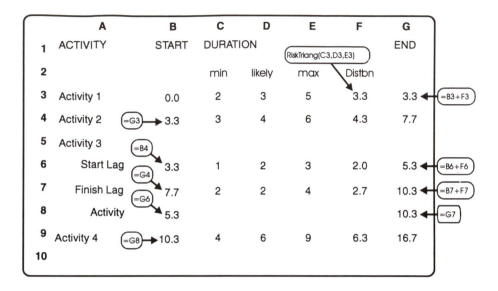

To convert the @RISK for Excel formulae shown here to @RISK for
Lotus 123 Release 2 replace:
    RiskTriang(A,B,C) with @TRIANG(A,B,C).

Figure 4.10 Model of network with lags and a passive activity

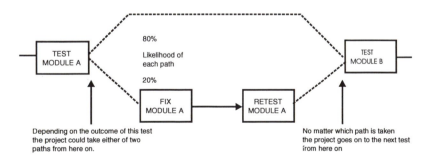

Figure 4.11 Network branching example

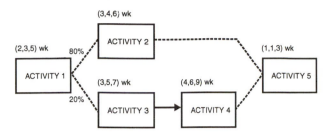

Figure 4.12   Network branching

represented in a schedule risk model. The most common branching points in normal IT projects are product selection decision points and the outcome of test and acceptance activities.

Figure 4.11 showed how branching can be represented graphically. What we need is a way to represent it in a risk model. One way is illustrated with Figures 4.12 and 4.13, a model network and its spreadsheet implementation.

In the model network the course of the project is uncertain at the end of activity 1. There is an 80% chance that it will go on to activity 2, the most likely outcome, and so the one on which plans are based. The alternative, with a likelihood of 20%, is that work will have to proceed through activity 3 and then activity 4, after which it will return to the expected path at activity 5.

The *@RISK* model of the network is shown in Figure 4.13. Compared with the other schedule risk models, it has one obvious difference: there is an extra column headed OCCURRENCE. The entries in the OCCURRENCE column indicate on each iteration of the model whether or not an activity occurs. Activities 1 and 5 will always occur, so their entries are blank. The occurrence of activity 2 is set to be true, signified by a value of 1, with a likelihood of 80%. When it is true the occurrence of activities 3 and 4, which are the same as one another, must be false, signified by a value of 0. Conversely, when activity 2 does not occur, activities 3 and 4 must do so. Whichever branch is followed, activity 5 starts when either 2 or 4 end.

The occurrence of an activity is set in the same way as the occurrence of a major risk in a cost model, using a discrete distribution with a value of 1 or 0. This is implemented in the model for activity 2 with a discrete distribution which will be 1 with a probability of 80% and 0 otherwise. The occurrence of the alternative path is calculated as 1 minus that of the main

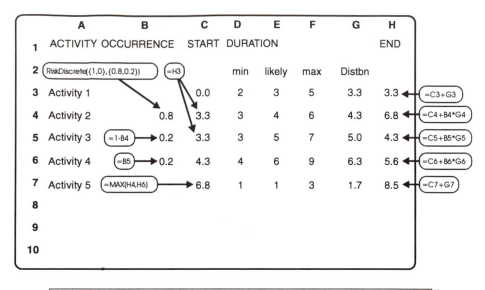

Figure 4.13 Model of network branching

path, for activity 3, and activities in the one path take their occurrence from the first one in the path, so activity 4 refers back to activity 3.

In the static spreadsheet the true average values of the cells are displayed, this is an option you can set in *@RISK*, so the occurrence of activity 2 is shown as 0.8. In fact during simulations it will be either 0 or 1, never anything in between.

We now have a means of flagging which activities occur. The model needs to use that information to calculate the activity end times which would arise in each case. This is achieved in the formulae for the activities start and end times.

With the activities which might not occur, the start times are calculated in the normal way, by referring to their predecessors. The impact of their occurrence is represented in their end times. Instead of calculating the end as the start plus the duration, it is calculated as the start plus the duration multiplied by the occurrence, as shown in Figure 4.13. This means that

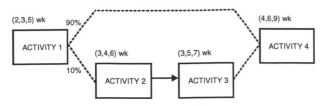

Figure 4.14 Unexpected work

anything which occurs is not affected; its end is its start plus its duration. Anything that does not occur has its duration cancelled out; its end equals its start.

The only remaining requirement is to ensure that the work following the branching point, activity 5 in this case, starts at the correct time. This is accomplished in the same way as for any activity with multiple predecessors, using the maximum of their ends. Activity 5 starts when the longest of the two branches finishes; this is the maximum of the end of activity 2 and the end of activity 4.

If a branching point is a major strategic decision, such as a fundamental choice of approach at the start of a project, the two branches might never rejoin. They might effectively represent two entirely different projects. They can always be rejoined in principle of course, by including a final activity, with no duration, called THE END or something similar, which starts when everything else is finished.

To illustrate the use of branching in more general circumstances, three more model networks and their spreadsheet implementations are shown in Figures 4.14–4.19. Only limited descriptions are given here, as they are simple extensions of the basic case and the diagrams are fully annotated.

Figure 4.14 shows the situation where unexpected work might be required. It is not an alternative to other activities, you expect to do nothing but know you might have to fix something. This is typical of test activity where you expect the tests to succeed but know that some bug fixes and retesting could be necessary. The model of this network is shown in Figure 4.15.

Figure 4.16 shows a network where the branches are more complex than in the first example. Within a branch, except for carrying the occurrence forward, the structure is just the same as for a conventional network. The model of this network is shown in Figure 4.17.

Figure 4.18 shows an uncommon but perfectly realistic situation where there is a branching point within a branch. The model of this network is shown in Figure 4.19. In this case the occurrences of activities in the second

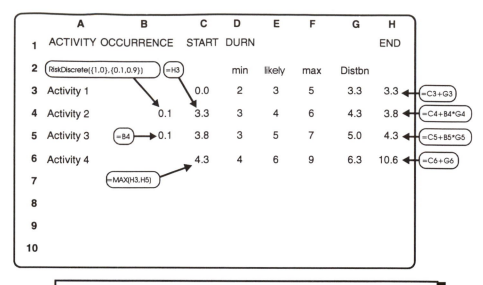

Figure 4.15 Model of unexpected work

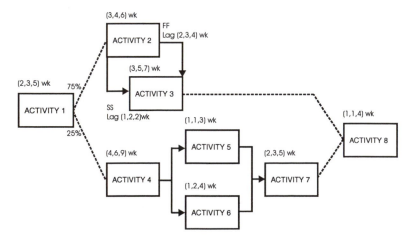

Figure 4.16 Complex branches

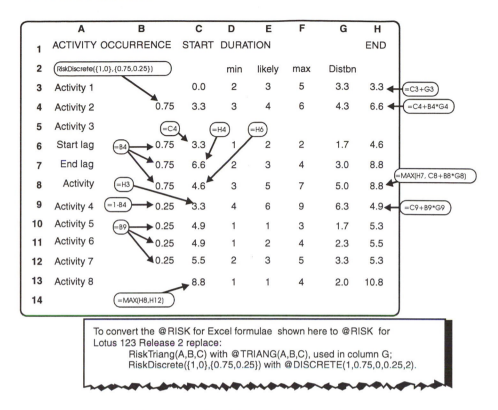

	A	B	C	D	E	F	G	H
1	ACTIVITY OCCURRENCE		START	DURATION				END
2	RiskDiscrete({1,0},{0.75,0.25})			min	likely	max	Distbn	
3	Activity 1		0.0	2	3	5	3.3	3.3 ◄─ =C3+G3
4	Activity 2	0.75	3.3	3	4	6	4.3	6.6 ◄─ =C4+B4*G4
5	Activity 3	=C4		=H4	=H6			
6	Start lag	=B4 0.75	3.3	1	2	2	1.7	4.6
7	End lag	0.75	6.6	2	3	4	3.0	8.8
8	Activity	=H3 0.75	4.6	3	5	7	5.0	8.8 ◄─ =MAX(H7, C8+B8*G8)
9	Activity 4	=1-B4 0.25	3.3	4	6	9	6.3	4.9 ◄─ =C9+B9*G9
10	Activity 5	=B9 0.25	4.9	1	1	3	1.7	5.3
11	Activity 6	0.25	4.9	1	2	4	2.3	5.5
12	Activity 7	0.25	5.5	2	3	5	3.3	5.3
13	Activity 8		8.8	1	1	4	2.0	10.8
14	=MAX(H8,H12)							

To convert the @RISK for Excel formulae shown here to @RISK for
Lotus 123 Release 2 replace:
RiskTriang(A,B,C) with @TRIANG(A,B,C), used in column G;
RiskDiscrete({1,0},{0.75,0.25}) with @DISCRETE(1,0.75,0,0.25,2).

Figure 4.17   Model of complex branches

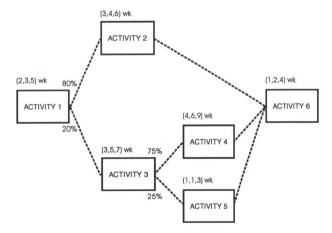

Figure 4.18   Multiple branches

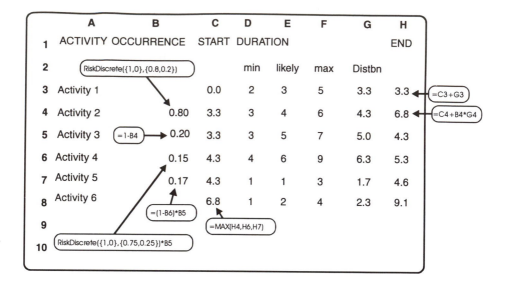

To convert the @RISK for Excel formulae shown here to @RISK for
Lotus 123 Release 2 replace:
  RiskTriang(A,B,C) with @TRIANG(A,B,C), used in column G;
  RiskDiscrete({1,0},{p,q}) with @DISCRETE(1,p,0,q,2).

Figure 4.19   Model of multiple branches

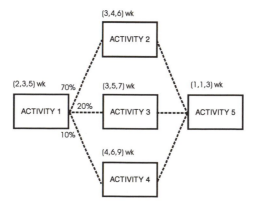

Figure 4.20   Three-way branching point

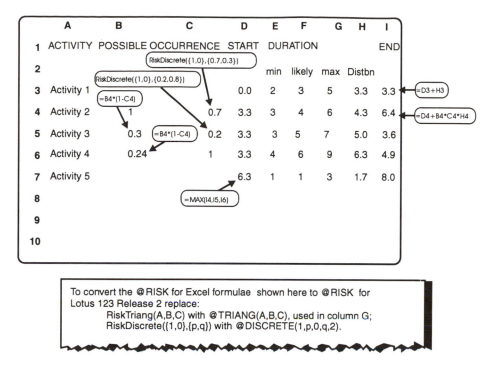

Figure 4.21 Model of three-way branching point

branch are multiplied by those of the first branch, to ensure that they only come into play if their overall branch occurs. Structures like this have a lot in common with decision trees, and can be nested as deeply as you wish. The most common reason for using one is where you cannot be sure that tests will be passed the second time around. It might be necessary to test, rework and retest several times.

It is most common to have two outcomes of an uncertain event, such as success and failure or acceptance and rejection. It is quite possible to have more, both in reality and in a model. For instance, the conclusion of trials on a new software product might be:

- complete acceptance, requiring no further work
- partial acceptance, requiring a degree of rework and retesting
- complete rejection, necessitating a search for an alternative.

Unless you are keen or think you might come across events with more than two outcomes, you can skip to the next part of this chapter on a first reading.

A model with three outcomes at a branching point is shown in Figure 4.20, and the model representing it is in Figure 4.21. The main difference from the previous models is the inclusion of another column. You can wrap up the interdependency between activities 2, 3 and 4 in complex occurrence formulae. However, these can become difficult to validate and edit. It is a lot easier to bring in the concept of an activity being possible, hence the new column.

If activity 2 occurs then neither 3 nor 4 is possible. If 2 does not occur and 3 does occur then 4 is not possible. Finally, if neither 2 nor 3 occurs, then 4 is both possible and in fact certain to occur. It is a lot easier to represent the possible outcomes using the twin concepts of possibility and occurrence than to use complicated formulae for the occurrence.

When the simulation is running and the first branch of this uncertain event, in row 4 of the spreadsheet, is being evaluated, nothing is fixed and the first branch is possible; it could occur. This means that the POSSIBLE entry for the first branch has a constant value of 1. Its OCCURRENCE entry is just the same as with a two-way branching point; it is a discrete distribution taking on the values 0 and 1 with appropriate probabilities.

The second branch will only be possible when the first does not occur, so its POSSIBLE entry is the POSSIBLE entry of the first branch multiplied by 1 minus the OCCURRENCE of the first branch. As an equation

$$P_2 = P_1(1 - O_1)$$

where P_i = the POSSIBLE entry for branch i, and O_i = the OCCURRENCE entry for branch i.

The occurrence of the second entry is another discrete distribution, with the appropriate probability of taking on a value of 1. The activity end is then calculated as the start plus the duration multiplied by both the occurrence and the possibility of the branch.

By flowing the relationship between a branch and the one which went before it down the list, you can have as many separate outcomes of an uncertain event as you wish. On any one iteration the first one to occur as evaluation moves through the list will block all those following it; their POSSIBLE entries all become 0 for that iteration. This goes on until you reach the last branch which has an OCCURRENCE entry with a constant value of 1. If this branch is possible, it means that none of the others occurred, so this one must occur.

It is your responsibility to ensure that the probabilities of multiple branches add up to 1. With a simple branching point it happens automatically if you use the structure described earlier. When there are three or more outcomes you have to work it out for yourself.

4.3.4 Correlation effects

Just as two or more uncertain costs might be correlated by dependence on a single underlying source of uncertainty, so might two or more activity durations. Some common sources of correlation between activity durations are:

- design, code and test activities, all depending on the complexity of a module's functionality

- several modules being driven by a common design or architectural feature, such as database size and complexity, product selection or communication network structure

- several activities being carried out by the one autonomous team, a subcontractor or part of a separate unit in your own organisation.

The search for correlation and the implications of ignoring it are identical to those discussed in Chapter 3. Once identified, the link between correlated activity durations is implemented in exactly the same way as for costs. The two special functions, *@INDEP* and *@DEP* in Lotus, and *RiskIndep* and *RiskDep* in Excel, are added to the triangular distributions used for the activity durations.

Where there is thought to be a straight ratio between the durations of activities, this too can be implemented in the way similar effects are handled in cost risk modelling. If, for instance, coding will take four times as long as design with the planned headcounts, then the coding duration can be represented by a simple formula which multiplies the design duration by four. This is equivalent to correlating the values, but depends on you formulating hard ratios between activities. It also means that you expect the same ratio between the three values in the three-point estimates of the two activities, which might not always be realistic. Design might be bound to take a minimum time because of consultations which are locked into a meeting schedule, for instance, while coding is relatively free of external constraints.

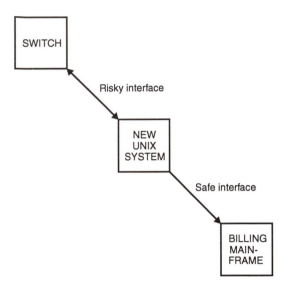

Figure 4.22 Outline system block diagram

4.3.5 Example schedule risk model

Background

An example schedule risk model is described here, based on part of a large project model developed in a real analysis. The project was to build a Unix system which would take call records from a telecommunications switch, process them and pass them on to a mainframe billing system, as illustrated in Figure 4.22. The switch and mainframe were already owned by the project's customer. The link to the mainframe was well understood and expected to cause few problems, as similar links to the same range of hardware had been implemented by the same team several times before. The link to the switch was more risky.

The switch hardware was relatively new and no one, not even the company who supplied it, had yet implemented a link of this sort to it. The project team knew that there could well be some discrepancies between the way the link protocol actually worked and the specifications on which they were basing their design. They also knew that if they uncovered a bug in the switch end of the link, only the switch supplier would be able to fix it.

There were several commercial and other reasons why the project anticipated less than perfect co-operation from the switch supplier. They had no direct hold over them and their customer had limited influence as the equipment was bought and paid for. The question was, how much trouble were they in?

Intitial plans

A first outline of the test activities is shown in Figure 4.23. It consists of three activities:

- protocol testing, to check that the link behaves as it should when it receives standard messages

- provocative testing, to check that it behaves sensibly when faced with erroneous messages

- volume testing, to make sure it will cope with the anticipated peak traffic levels.

Each stage was expected to take about a week. Provocative testing was to start when protocol testing ended, and volume testing was to start a week later, ending one week after provocative testing finished.

The logical connection between the second and third stages could have been shown as a FS link without affecting the overall duration of the test activity. The SS and FF linkage is retained because it represents the true dependency of the activities, and in what follows this becomes important.

Figure 4.23 suggests a three-week test phase, but the team knew it was risky and wanted to add a contingency to the schedule. Bearing in mind that people tend to think of contingencies in terms of 5 to 20%, the team

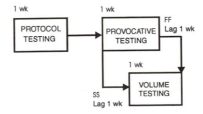

Figure 4.23   First view of test activities

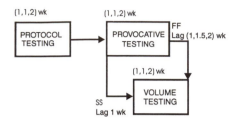

Figure 4.24 Uncertainty in test activity durations

thought they would stick their necks out and suggest a 33% contingency for this activity, an extra week. As the project was under pressure on timescales, this was not a decision to be taken lightly.

Risk model

The whole project network was subjected to a risk analysis, but as this test activity was particularly complex, risky and fell near the end of the project, it was analysed separately in detail. The first thing to consider was the uncertainty in the durations of the activities and lags in Figure 4.23. The three-point estimates which replaced the original estimates are shown in Figure 4.24.

As these activities were all to be carried out by the one team with the one set of software, it was expected that there would be a strong link between the speed of operation throughout the tests. All these activities were correlated with one another. If it had not been for the concern about the link to the switch, the model might have been developed no further.

When the consequences of a bug at the switch end of the link were explored, it became clear that three branching points needed to be added to the model. At the end of each test stage there was a risk of needing to ask the switch manufacturer to correct bugs in the link handler. The likelihood of this happening was assessed as 1 in 3 at each stage, quite high. If it happened, the work would be delayed until the bug was rectified; then a little rework at our end of the link and repeat tests would be necessary. It was thought unlikely that secondary bugs would arise from the fix. The network that represents the test activity with all this branching is shown in Figure 4.25.

The time allowed for the switch manufacturer to correct bugs at each stage was very uncertain. It was thought unlikely that, even with the best will in the world, the work could be taken on and turned around in less than one week. However, given the lack of influence, let alone control,

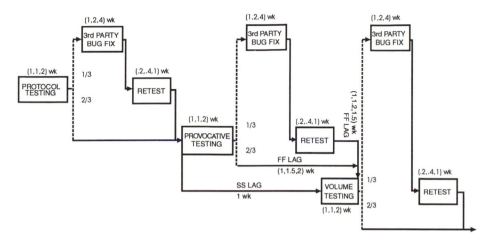

Figure 4.25 Uncertainty in network logic and durations

over this activity, it was thought that a reluctant supplier could take up to four weeks without appearing to be unreasonable. On the whole it was expected that a bug fix would be most likely to take two weeks. Finally, it was expected that if more than one set of bugs had to be fixed, the same degree of co-operation, or lack of it, would be forthcoming on each occasion. This was represented by correlating the estimates for the switch bug fixing activities with one another.

Even before the model was evaluated, this picture and the identification of the strong correlations between the two groups of activities gave a much clearer picture of the problem facing the project during these tests. It helped the team understand their task and communicate it to their management.

Results

The output of the model is shown in Figure 4.26. The original plan, allowing a budget of four weeks, was obviously optimistic, even though it had been considered pushy to include a 33% contingency. In fact the project needed to be prepared to spend around 9 or 10 weeks in testing this link.

Managerially this could be handled in two ways. The project could have built in a planned duration of around nine weeks and accepted this as a realistic target. However, a different approach was taken. A target of six weeks was taken as being possible, although risky, thus setting

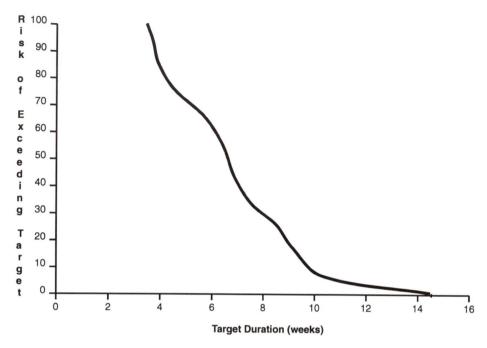

Figure 4.26 Test activity model output

expectations at the low end of the range. The project manager retained a contingency of a further three weeks to cover the risk associated with the tests.

Conventional methods would not have brought the project team, or their management, to a realistic understanding of the risk in this situation. The sequence of events, with three branching points, and the correlation between activities is too much for the unaided human brain to assess reliably.

Quite apart from the complexity of the network logic, the normal expectations of test activities and acceptable contingency levels forced everyone towards an optimistic assessment of the duration. Only a clear documented analysis was able to break through this expectation, which in this case was unrealistic. The novelty of the link protocol and the commercial relationship between the project and the switch supplier, or lack of it, were both extraordinary.

Experience breaks down when we face extraordinary circumstances, and we can never be sure how badly it is failing, unless we get back to a level at which we do understand what is going on. In this case that level was the individual stages of the test. Each one and the outcomes following it were fairly easy to describe. It was the overall picture which could not be assessed reliably without a model.

The model took only an hour or so to build, for the test activity alone. This represents a small investment against the problems which would arise, both internal to the contractor and in their relations with the customer, if a key step in the project took 100% longer than expected. The analysis allowed expectations to be set at realistic levels before it became an issue.

4.4 INTERPRETING SCHEDULE RISK MODEL OUTPUT

Schedule risk model output shows the same features as cost risk model output, plus a few more. As with cost risk models, the best and worst case possible will usually fall outside the realistically likely range of outcomes. Where there is any correlation between durations in the model, the range of uncertainty will be greater than it would otherwise have been. An estimate calculated from the most likely values of the constituent parts generally has less than a 50/50 chance of being achieved, because the most likely values are nearer the minimum of each uncertain quantity than the maximum. These features are common to all risk models.

Schedule models have one major characteristic which sets them apart from simple cost and other financial models, this is the network relationship between their elements. The structure of the network affects the relationship between the uncertainty in separate activities and the uncertainty in a whole project. Two main issues need to be borne in mind when interpreting the results of a schedule risk model, nodes in the network and branching points.

4.4.1 Nodes

Figure 4.27 shows the output of the model illustrated in Figure 4.6, a simple network of four activities. If you take the most likely duration of each activity in the network, you would calculate a network duration of 14 weeks, a target with a 70% risk of being exceeded. This is more than just the effect of the most likely values of each activity being nearer the low end of the range than the top.

Activity 4 cannot start until both 2 and 3 are complete, so the network always reflects the worst case. It is driven by the longest of the two parallel activities, ending at the node which is the start of activity 4. This effect is

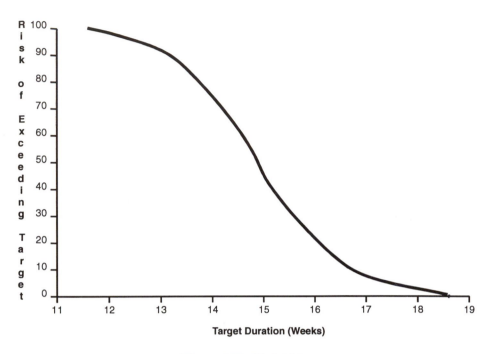

Figure 4.27 Nodal bias

accentuated in real networks, where there might be more than two activities coming together at a node, and there are usually several nodes.

To obtain a feel for the effect of nodes, think about an activity with four predecessors. If each one has just a 10% chance of finishing late, what is the chance of the successor starting on time? For this to happen each of the predecessors must end on time, events with a probability of 90%. The chance of four independent events happening when each one has a separate chance of 90% is $0.9^4 = 0.66$, a risk of failure of over 1 in 3. A risk which was being described in terms of numbers around 10% is three times greater simply because of the logical relationship between activities.

This effect is sometimes described as nodal bias. In real networks it can be so severe that a project duration calculated from most likely values has almost no chance of being achieved. You can obtain some feel for the extent to which your plans will suffer from nodal bias by looking at the network logic. The more nodes and the greater the number of predecessors at each one, the more severe the effect is likely to be. Integration, test and acceptance activities tend to be the worst affected in IT projects. Any steps

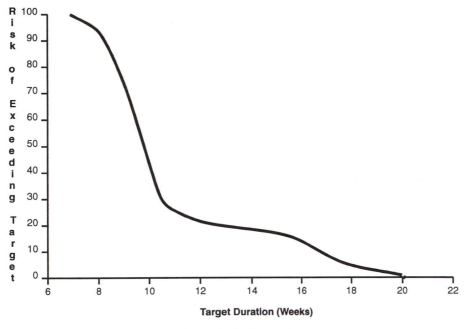

Figure 4.28 Branching

you can take to soften the nodal structure will reduce your risk, both in the model and in reality.

4.4.2 Branching

Figure 4.28 shows the output of the model in Figure 4.12, a simple example of branching. The main difference between this and figure 4.27 is the way in which the slope of the graph changes. Instead of starting with a shallow slope at the left, becoming steeper in the middle and then flattening off, this curve has a flat section in the middle too.

This curve can be thought of as two ordinary curves blended together. The left-hand portion represents the short path with an 80% probability. This fades out around a duration of 12 weeks. At about 14 weeks the curve for the longer path, with a probability of 20%, comes into play.

If your project takes the short path it is almost certain to have been completed before week 12, but if it takes the longer path it is unlikely to have been completed until several weeks later. This means that there is little point setting your target in the flat region; it will either be easy or impossible. Faced with such a profile there are two ways to plan: you can set a target based on the short path and a contingency to allow for the long path; or you can set a target and contingency based on the long path, and work to take the opportunity to do a lot better. Which you choose will depend on motivations, politics and commercial arrangements.

In real networks individual branches are likely to be lost in the general uncertainty, as there will usually be other activities in parallel with both the alternative paths. However, if your model does show a flat section in its output, the branches are likely to be the cause. Anything strong enough to show up in the model as a whole is likely to be an important feature of your project, worthy of special attention in planning and management.

4.5 HUMAN FACTORS

All the issues which stand in the way of obtaining realistic data about uncertainty in cost estimates, described in Chapter 3, apply equally well to schedule risk assessment. In addition to these there are two particular areas where human factors enter into schedule risk assessment and need to be borne in mind. These are expectations of the maximum durations of the activities and the revision of plans to limit the risk of an over-run.

4.5.1 Maximum durations of activities

There is a common tendency, especially among people who have been convinced that they must 'think positive', to be unwilling to accept that an activity might take longer than planned. To the question 'What is the maximum time it could take?', they respond with 'It will be finished in the planned time, it will not be allowed to take longer', or words to that effect. The words 'it will not be allowed to take longer' or 'it must not take any longer' are so consistent that they must reflect a common feature of the way businesses manage their staff.

While most people are willing to accept that costs could exceed expectations, and might even take a perverse delight in recounting past examples, the same is not true of deadlines. This is probably due to the fact that cost over-runs are resolved in-house, while schedule issues are open and visible to the customer.

There might be ways in which a schedule can be held no matter what happens. Study tasks are almost always finished on time because the scope of work is allowed to vary according to what the study turns up. This is the exception rather than the rule though. In general you can only be sure that a task will finish on time if:

- the scope of work is flexible, at least to some extent

- it will be possible to calibrate the task from the early part of the work, to tell if the planned work rate is adequate

- you can raise the work rate and/or reduce the scope of work to bring the task back on target in the time left after you find it is heading for an over-run.

Consider an example. You need to convert about 100 old COBOL modules into a new environment in 25 weeks, each one will take about 1 person-week of effort and the conversion team is four-strong.

Let us assume that after eight weeks you find that only 20 modules have been converted, instead of the 32 or so you would expect, and there is no reason to believe that progress will improve markedly in the future. The average effort per module is 1.6 person-weeks. Instead of 100 person-weeks of work you are looking at a total of 160, with 32 spent, leaving 128 to go. This task is either going to take 60% longer than expected or require additional staff. This is a simple example of earned value or CSCS/C analysis (Turner, 1993).

Now let us be optimistic and imagine that you can persuade the team to work an extra day per week or the equivalent in longer days. Ignoring the effect of the overtime on your costs, this is equivalent to having 4.8 staff. At the rate of 1.6 person-weeks per module there is $80 \times 1.6/4.8 = 27$ weeks of work to be completed in the remaining 17 weeks. Even with the overtime you need extra staff.

In calculating the number of new staff you need it is important to allow for:

- the time it will take to find them

- the time they will need to come up to speed, learning about your project and the work to be done

- the amount of the existing team's time required to induct and train the new recruits.

This is illustrated in Figure 4.29. The problem we now face was described in the renowned book *The Mythical Man-Month* (Brooks, 1974).

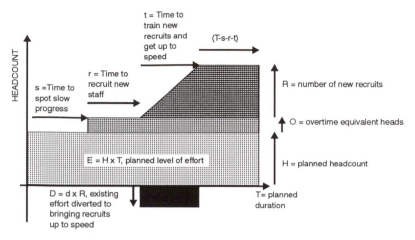

Figure 4.29 Responding to an underestimate

A simple geometric equation derived from the diagram in Figure 4.29 shows that the number of extra staff required to finish a job on time is

$$R = (A - HT - O(T - s))/(T - s - r - 0.5t - dt)$$

where

A = the actual effort required to complete the task
H = the headcount allocated in the original plan
T = the planned duration
O = the effective number of heads supplied by overtime working
R = the number of new heads recruited
s = the time it takes to realise that progress is slower than planned
r = the time it takes to recruit new staff
t = the time it takes the new staff to get up to speed and become fully productive
d = the proportion of an experienced person's effort required to support a new recruit during the training period

In the current example, if we assume that you can obtain new staff in four weeks and they need two weeks to come up to speed, absorbing 20% of someone else's time as they do so, you need four new staff to achieve the deadline, doubling the team size!

If anyone claims that their schedule is fireproof they should be able to go through an argument like this to prove it, using cost or effort estimates to assess the scale of any potential over-run. By putting A equal to the maximum effort estimate, you can assess the project's capacity to contain an over-run in key activities.

In practice most people find that by the time they have discovered they are heading for an over-run, there is little or no chance of getting new effort onto the task quickly enough to make any difference. The time it takes to recognise a problem, the time required to recruit new staff, the time they take to come up to speed and the drain on your existing team while they are being trained, all tend to be greater than you would think. This means that the idea of a task which 'cannot be allowed to over-run', is usually wishful thinking.

Even if someone can demonstrate that it would be possible to detect the potential over-run, and respond in time to safeguard the schedule, it means nothing unless the project management plan includes explicit measures to ensure that it will happen. There would have to be an effective mechanism to monitor progress, not just spend, an identified source of additional staff and clear contingency plans for bringing them on board cost-effectively when required. Only then could you hope that an over-run would 'not be allowed to happen'.

On short tasks, around four weeks long, even with progress monitoring it is unlikely to be possible to detect and correct slow progress on any significant scale. In general, the only safe risk management strategy to contain an over-run is to apply sufficient resources at the outset to finish on time with the worst-case effort requirement. You then have an opportunity to release staff if the worst case is not realised, or to finish ahead of time, building up a schedule contingency for the project.

None of the preceding discussion is concerned with major risks, merely the danger of having made an optimistic estimate. In most cases you cannot accept assertions that schedule slippage will not be allowed to happen. Duration estimates must include a realistic level of uncertainty. How you design the work programme to safeguard key milestones is then a separate matter, discussed in the next section.

4.5.2 Planning to reduce schedule risk

If you have used realistic assessments of the uncertainty in activities' durations, and a model of the whole project shows a high risk of exceeding the required end date, what do you do about it? Broadly speaking there are three ways out:

- change the technical solution to something which can be achieved more quickly, possibly at additional cost

- add extra resources to complete tasks more quickly

- run in parallel activities which were in series.

Radical changes of plan are rarely on offer. Adding more resources is sometimes possible, but there are tasks which cannot be broken down and parcelled out to armies of people to get them finished more quickly. There are also cost penalties arising from additional induction, training and management as more and more people are assigned to a project.

The most common response to schedule risk is to place activities in parallel when you would rather they were in series. In an ideal world, design work would always be complete before coding began, with all interactions between parts of the design identified and resolved. In practice they almost always overlap. This means that late design changes can require early coding to be reworked. There is nothing wrong with this of course, so long as everyone understands the situation at the outset, and makes appropriate allowance for the rework.

Cost and schedule three-point estimates usually take into account the uncertain complexity and scale of a task. They rarely allow for the fact that some effort will be wasted because activities are being run in parallel. The worst-case estimate should really allow for the worst complexity, the greatest scale and the highest level of rework which can realistically be expected. The more activities are overlapped the greater the allowance you need to make. Every time the network logic is changed to shorten a project plan, you need to review the estimates, especially the maximum values, to check that they are still realistic.

4.6 EXTERNAL DEPENDENCIES

It is one thing to build a plan based on the estimates and commitments of people in the same immediate business organisation as youself. Several issues arise when your project depends on subcontractors, or even other parts of your own company.

As you develop your plans and risk models the commitment of your subcontractors, whether internal or external to your organisation, could range from almost nothing to a signed contract. People often think that once a subcontractor is committed to providing something by a certain date the main project is free of risk in that area. A moment's thought shows that this is not so.

In the extreme, suppose that your subcontractor goes out of business. What happens to your schedule? You are still responsible to your customer for the project being finished on time. You can sue the subcontractor, but even if there is money to be recouped in this way it will rarely bring the project back on schedule as legal proceedings take a long time. Your project retains a risk in the areas where you subcontract the work and there is no way out of it.

Having reluctantly accepted that you cannot divest yourself of risk through subcontracts, how do you assess the uncertainty? Once again there is a tendency to think that this task has now been handed off to the subcontractor. In practice it is rare to get information about uncertainty from a subcontractor, unless you are working in a very close partnership with them. As in all other aspects of risk assessment it is the people who carry the risk who must produce or at least approve the estimates. You have to take your own view of the risk associated with a task, even if it has been subcontracted. This is the only view which matters. It might be informed by other people, but it has to be something you believe, if you are going to use the information to make decisions.

A subcontractor's plans might provide a starting point, but if they relate only to a loose commitment you might ignore them entirely, and put in what you really expect to happen. Your assessment might be that the subcontractor is being optimistic. During bidding you will often need to consider the possibility of a different subcontractor actually carrying out the work when you get around to making firm deals. It is quite common to have to allow for a subcontractor defaulting, through technical incompetence, bankruptcy, loss of key staff or other difficulties. All of these need to be your view and are easily represented in the same way as the rest of the project network, with linked activities, three-point estimates and branching points.

4.7 SELLING CONFIDENCE

The customer representative who evaluates your proposal is generally a supplier within his or her own organisation. These people have commitments to meet and deadlines to be achieved. A risk assessment of the schedule of your proposal is a powerful means of giving your customer confidence in your commitments.

Even if a bid is to be vetted by the Chief Executive of a company, she or he has shareholders to satisfy. Your customers need confidence that what they are being offered will be delivered on time. Inclusion of a simple risk model in your proposal can illustrate where the main risks lie, show how they are to be managed and even enlist customer support in controlling them. Assuming that you have been able to come up with a low-risk plan, a model is the easiest way to demonstrate its value to your customers, value for which they will pay.

5

BUSINESS FORECAST RISK

5.1 BUSINESS FORECAST UNCERTAINTY

Every business forecasts future activity, to make or validate plans, decide on investment and set a baseline for monitoring and control. If your income comes from selling baked beans, torch batteries or other mass-produced items, there could be literally millions of individual sales each year going to make up your income. With such vast numbers of sales, the individual details of each one are irrelevant.

A project-based business needs to forecast just as much as any other, but it faces special problems in doing so. Instead of millions of low-value opportunities which can be treated as a statistical population, there are likely to be tens or even fewer high-value opportunities, each of which must be considered separately. Each opportunity is unique and independent of the others. Forecasting in a projects business has to allow for the characteristics of each separate major opportunity.

Project business forecasting relies heavily on experienced judgement, and it always will. However, the application of some simple modelling techniques can give experienced managers better information, and help others find their way through what can be a minefield.

5.2 CONVENTIONAL APPROACHES TO FORECASTING

Project business managers can usually list the opportunities they are now or could in future be bidding to win, as well as those they have already won. For each one identified it is possible to specify, if only roughly, the net cash flow to date and the expected future cost and revenue, both in the current accounting period and annually for the next few years if the projects span more than one year. The conventional approach to forecasting end of year profit and other business performance measures is effectively a subjective examination of this list.

A little quantitative uncertainty might creep into the analysis if opportunities yet to be won are allocated a win probability, and this is used to discount their contributions. The simplicity of this approach is appealing, but it can oversimplify a complex situation. You might win 1 in 3 of the opportunities with a 1 in 3 win probability, but how near the end of the year will your customers sign the contracts, for instance? A contract taken in the last few months of the year can cost more than it earns by the time the books are closed for the current year.

Most project-based businesses actually fall part-way between the simple view, where all the available opportunities are identified, and the volume market, where opportunities are treated *en masse*. Individual opportunities can usually be identified some way into the future, but not beyond a certain point.

For instance, small consultancy contracts rarely come to light much more than a month or two before a bid is due, and are awarded soon after bids are received. An annual forecast for such a business will be a mixture of identified opportunities and broad assessments of the remaining potential of each market segment. It might not be possible to separate out individual opportunities beyond the next few months, but estimates can be made of the overall level and profitability of operations in each area.

Current practice is generally for all forecasts to be expressed as single values, with all the drawbacks this approach brings to project cost and schedule estimating. It takes little extra work to describe both the general level of and the uncertainty in forecasts, as set out in the next part of this chapter.

5.3 DESCRIBING PROJECT BUSINESS FORECASTS

5.3.1 Specific and general opportunities

An identified opportunity can be described in terms of the chance of winning it, its start date, value and duration. Each of these can be directly represented in a model. General unidentified opportunities need to be estimated as a whole, or market segment by market segment. The

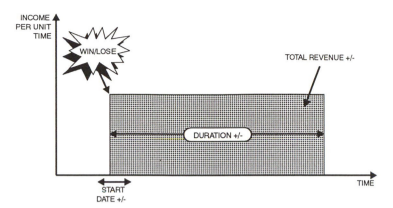

Figure 5.1 Uncertainty in revenue from a single project

representation of these two types of business is set out in the next two sections.

5.3.2 Describing identified opportunities

The conventional approach to forecasting project business wastes a lot of information which is there waiting to be exploited. To understand what this information is, and how to use it, think about the major uncertainties in the forecast of a single project, at the business level. The main questions during forecasting are:

- will we win it?

- when will work start?

- how much will it be worth, in revenue and margin?

- how long will it go on, and so how thinly will the money be spread over the months?

These come down to one event, win/lose, and some relatively simple timing and value issues. All of them can be described using the same building blocks as the cost and schedule models in the last two chapters. Win/lose uncertainty is a simple uncertain event, and the others are uncertain values. Figure 5.1 illustrates the uncertainty in a single opportunity's revenue, where the revenue profile can be assumed to be roughly flat.

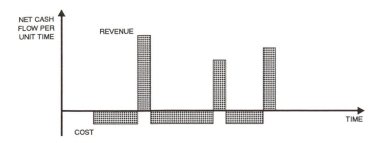

Figure 5.2 Cash flow per unit time

Where there are many opportunities, and payment terms are such as to give a roughly neutral cash flow on any one project, the simple model in Figure 5.1 is probably sufficient to represent a project. Margin can be described by an uncertain value, a distribution, and used to calculate profit from the revenue.

Most businesses focus on true cash flow, rather than revenue and assumptions about the margin. Where you want allow for the actual cash flow profiles of individual opportunities, it requires only a little extra complexity in the model. To a first approximation, the cost profiles of many projects can be assumed to be flat, especially when effort constitutes the bulk of the cost. Revenue tends to be pegged to payment milestones and received in lump sums. A typical cash flow profile of this type is illustrated in Figure 5.2.

The refinement of the cash flow model of each opportunity can be extended as far as you like. If the cost profile cannot be assumed to be uniform it can either be described with a more complex shape, as in Figure 5.3, or approximated by a set of uniform segments, as in Figure 5.4.

In the modelling section below only the simple case shown in Figure 5.1 is used. This will generally be sufficient, and if greater detail is required the structure can easily be extended to accommodate it.

Where stage payments, or any other cash flow which occurs as lump sums, are important, they can easily be accommodated in the same structure. This is explained in the section on profile modelling.

5.3.3 Describing the general opportunities

The simplest way to represent the general opportunities, those yet to be specifically identified, is simply to estimate the revenue or profit they will yield as a single uncertain value. You might have identified all the

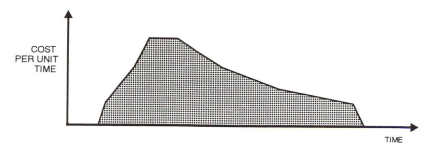

Figure 5.3 Forecast cost per unit time

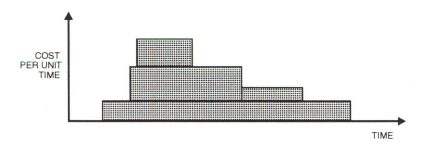

Figure 5.4 Uniform segments approximating forecast cash flow

opportunities that could start up to three months from now, and have a single estimate representing the revenue you expect to generate beyond that point, to the end of the year, for instance.

Forecasts are often broken down by market segment, based on product type, customer, geographical region or some other characteristics. If you already describe your forecasts in terms of market segments, it obviously makes sense to estimate the revenue or profit separately, with a three-point estimate, for each segment in each time period.

5.3.4 Correlations

Correlation is one of the most critical and frequently overlooked aspects of risk models. It is just as important to business forecasting as to any other field. If two or more components of your business are driven by the one underlying factor, they need to be linked in your model to ensure that it is realistic.

It might be that the award dates of two or more projects are correlated by a policy decision of a government department to limit spending by slowing the rate at which contracts are let. If you are entering a new market, or have several opportunities based on one new product or new working practice, your forecasts of the margins on related opportunities might be correlated. Business is too complex to anticipate all the correlations which could arise. You need to think through the issues for yourself, using your own knowledge of your business and all the influences on it.

5.4 BUSINESS FORECAST RISK MODELS

5.4.1 Profiles

The representation of uncertain events and values has been thoroughly covered in the preceding chapters. One new issue arises in business forecasting, though: the issue of time. Time obviously came into schedule modelling, but only in terms of the overall duration of a project. However, business forecasting is not only concerned with how much something is worth over all, or how long it will take from start to end. It is crucially concerned with the month-by-month profile of cash flow, in and out.

The reason that the start date of a new project is so important, for instance, is that it affects the amount of profit you can expect to generate in the current accounting period. Annual results often dominate business decision-making, and are very important for individual business managers.

Since we are concerned with the cash flow and how it will be distributed between time periods, these time periods need to be represented in the model. This is the main new component of a business forecasting model, compared with cost and schedule models: the inclusion of a time profile.

5.4.2 Overall model structure

The overall structure of a business forecast risk model is illustrated in Figure 5.5, in block form. The particular case shown here is a profit model.

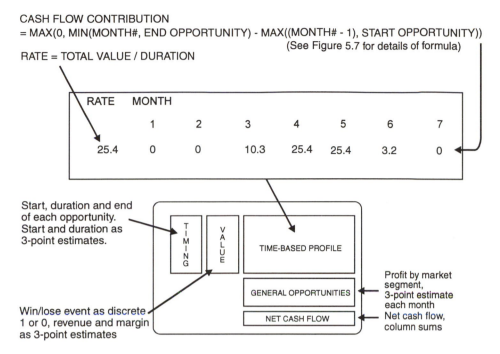

CASH FLOW CONTRIBUTION
= MAX(0, MIN(MONTH#, END OPPORTUNITY) - MAX((MONTH# - 1), START OPPORTUNITY))
(See Figure 5.7 for details of formula)
RATE = TOTAL VALUE / DURATION

RATE	MONTH						
	1	2	3	4	5	6	7
25.4	0	0	10.3	25.4	25.4	3.2	0

Start, duration and end of each opportunity. Start and duration as 3-point estimates.

TIMING

VALUE

TIME-BASED PROFILE

GENERAL OPPORTUNITIES

NET CASH FLOW

Win/lose event as discrete 1 or 0, revenue and margin as 3-point estimates

Profit by market segment, 3-point estimate each month

Net cash flow, column sums

Figure 5.5 Profit model outline structure

The model consists of four main blocks, representing timing, value, time-based profiles and the contributions of general opportunities.

The timing block sets out the start, duration and end of each identified opportunity. The start dates and durations will generally be represented by distributions based on three-point estimates, and the end dates will be calculated by adding them together. All of these will need to be expressed in units compatible with the time base of the profile, generally weeks, months, quarters or years relative to the start of the current year. So if a contract is due to be awarded between the start of April and the end of July, but most probably in mid-May, its start date could be described by the three-point estimate (3, 4.5, 7), in months from the start of the current year. Both the start and the duration of each opportunity are taken into account, because the longer a job drags on, the slower the profit will be in coming in.

The value block represents the revenue value and percentage margin of each opportunity. It is perfectly simple to enter profit directly as an uncertain value, but the information to hand is usually the expected price range of each opportunity and an expectation of margin, based on the type of business you are in. The margin and revenue values are used to calculate the profit, which then embodies the uncertainty in both the quantities from which it is derived. Construction of a model directly in terms of the concepts used to describe the business, revenue and margin in this case, helps to make a model easy to understand.

The profile block is described in more detail in the next section. It performs two tasks. Firstly, it calculates a rate at which profit is to be accrued. In the simple model it assumes a flat profile, so the rate is uniform from the start to the end of one opportunity. The rest of the profile block consists of a column for each time period, in which the profit contribution of each opportunity is spread out over time.

The final part of the model, the fourth block, simply provides a place for the estimated profit from as yet unidentified opportunities to be set out in time, represented by three-point estimates. These are direct estimates for each of the market segments. It is probably worth considering the possibility that all your monthly forecasts in any particular market segment could be correlated with one another. Either the same business conditions will affect them all, or your view might have been uniformly optimistic or pessimistic across a whole segment.

5.4.3 Profile modelling

The only part of the profit model illustrated in Figure 5.5 that is markedly different from those in earlier chapters is the profile block. This calculates the cash flow of each identified opportunity in each time period covered by the model. Addition of the individual contributions to obtain the net cash flow in each period is simple; the trick is to calculate them in the first place.

The profit contribution of an opportunity to a time period, within a single iteration of a model, depends on the rate at which it accrues and on how much the opportunity and the time period overlap. The six types of overlap which could arise, for a single opportunity and single time period, are illustrated in Figure 5.6. It is possible to set up formulae using IF statements to determine which of these six possibilities applies, and to calculate the contribution of an opportunity accordingly. Such formulae become rather long, though, and they slow down the iterative evaluation of models. There is a simpler alternative which allows models to run faster, and is easier to set up and edit. Figure 5.7 illustrates a formula which will calculate the amount of time an opportunity overlaps with a particular time period.

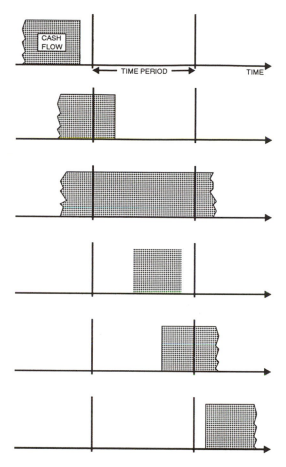

Figure 5.6 Possible relationships between an accounting period and a cash flow element

All the key formulae required for profit modelling are shown in Figures 5.5 and 5.7. The rate at which each opportunity contributes profit is calculated by dividing the total contribution by the total duration of an opportunity. This is multiplied by the overlap to calculate the net contribution in each time period.

This structure can be used to represent any profile, by feeding in an appropriate rate. The changes necessary to represent the revenue of a set of opportunities should be fairly obvious. If you are concerned about resource demand, the headcount of each opportunity, expressed as a three-point estimate, can be used as the rate to give an assessment of the uncertainty in the total resource demand profile for the business over time.

Lump sum costs and payments are easily accommodated in such a model. Although lump sum cash flows happen in an instant, when they do happen they can be given a notional short duration, say one day. This translates into a very high rate in terms of £/month, but since it also gives a very short overlap with the relevant time period, around 0.03 months, this is cancelled out. Using this approach it is possible to keep the structure of each line in the profile block the same, making it simple to build and maintain the model.

5.4.4 Example

Table 5.1 shows the data for a profit model of a small- to medium-sized projects business. It represents a half-year position, with some business in hand and several opportunities which might or might not be won. There is also some as yet unidentified business which is expected to be won before the year is out, represented directly as forecast profit contributions.

These models tend to become a bit more extensive than project cost and schedule models, so no attempt has been made to show the whole

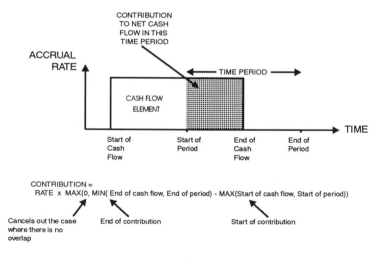

Figure 5.7 Formula for calculating the contribution of a cash flow element in a particular accounting period

Table 5.1 Profit risk assessment example data

| Oppor-tunity | Win probability | Schedule (months from 1 January) | | | | | | End |
| | | Start | | | Duration | | | |
		min.	likely	max.	min.	likely	max.	
1	1.0		6.0		2.0	3.0	5.0	9.3
2	1.0		6.0		6.0	7.0	9.0	13.3
3	0.3	7.0	8.0	10.0	4.0	4.0	5.0	12.7
4	0.4	6.5	7.0	8.0	2.0	2.5	3.5	9.8
5	0.2	7.0	7.0	9.0	3.0	3.0	5.0	11.3
6	0.4	7.0	8.0	11.0	2.0	2.0	3.0	11.0
7	0.4	6.0	7.0	8.5	2.0	3.0	5.0	10.5
8	0.5	7.5	8.0	10.0	3.0	3.5	4.5	12.2

PROFIT TO DATE   £800 thousand

| Oppor-tunity | Value £ thousand | | | | | |
| | Revenue | | | Margin (fraction) | | |
	min.	likely	max.	min.	likely	max.
1	400	450	525	0.14	0.18	0.21
2	375	480	550	0.17	0.22	0.26
3	525	600	780	0.14	0.18	0.21
4	625	700	800	0.14	0.18	0.21
5	250	300	370	0.17	0.22	0.26
6	425	475	550	0.14	0.18	0.21
7	480	500	550	0.17	0.22	0.26
8	550	600	700	0.17	0.22	0.26

Oppor-tunity	Profile			Time periods		
				Q3	Q4	
	Profit rate £ thousand/ month	From end month	6	9	Year
		To end month	9	12	end
1	24.3			72.9	8.1	81.0
2	13.8			41.5	41.5	83.0
3	7.8			5.2	23.3	28.5
4	18.8			34.4	15.6	50.1
5	3.6			4.8	8.5	13.3
6	14.6			4.9	29.3	34.2
7	13.3			24.3	19.9	44.2
8	18.2			9.1	54.7	63.8

| Segment | Q3 | | | Q4 | | |
	min.	likely	max.	min.	likely	max.
A	100	150	160	75	90	100
B	120	150	160	100	110	110

Opportunities 1 and 2 are already running.

There are two major market segments. The profit expected from them in each of the next two quarters is represented by these three-point estimates.

For each segment the estimates for Q3 and Q4 are correlated.

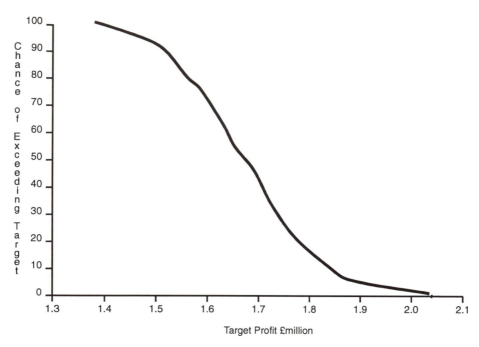

Figure 5.8 Profit opportunity profile

thing here. Its general form was described earlier in this chapter, and the results of the model are shown in Figure 5.8.

This business could reliably commit itself to generating around £1.5 million profit in the current year on these predictions. There is an opportunity to make more, of course, but as you would expect, the higher the target, the greater the risk that it will not be achieved.

5.4.5 Interpreting results

In common with project cost and schedule risk assessments, business forecast risk assessments fall somewhere between statistical probabilities and measures of difficulty. The output of the model is an indication of what could happen, not a prediction of what will happen. It can be used to help decide what target to set, or to illustrate what is required to meet a target which has been imposed or agreed earlier.

The labels on the model output are slightly different from those of project cost and schedule risk models. The vertical axis is the likelihood of

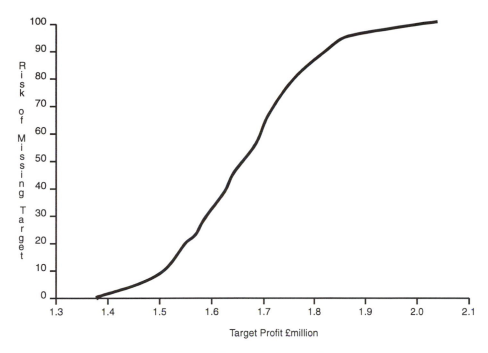

Figure 5.9 Profit risk profile

achieving at least as much as the target, not the risk of missing it. The curve could be plotted the other way up, as in Figure 5.9, to represent the risk of missing the target, if you wished.

In this case the easy targets are at the left-hand end of the graph and the tough targets are at the right, whichever way up the graph is plotted. The level of risk at which you decide to set and accept targets is a very personal matter. There will generally be more flexibility in a business as a whole than in a single project, so there is always a chance that a bright idea could generate more income than expected. The output of a model will never give you a definitive prediction, but it will tell you which ball park you are in and indicate how hard it is going to be to hit your targets.

There are no simple rules about the level of risk at which to pitch business targets. It is important to remember that a model can only help you understand the business. The rest is down to experience and judgement, as it always has been.

In addition to the model's output, there is scope to use the data you feed into it, to help improve your understanding of the business it represents. An examination of the data in Table 5.1 will show where the greatest uncertainty lies, which opportunities it affects and whether it has most to do with their timing, their value or the chances of winning. Different action is likely to be taken to nudge each of these in your favour.

5.5 HUMAN FACTORS

Any discussion of risk raises a lot of complex personal issues, some of which have been discussed in the preceding two chapters. The commitment demanded of business managers is likely to be even greater than that asked of most project managers. If a project goes off the rails, the project manager is likely to suffer, but will not always bear the consequences of circumstances seen to be beyond the project's control, especially on smaller projects. The whole point of business management is to succeed in spite of volatility in the market.

The technical issues in business forecasting are the same as in project assessment, but personal factors take on greater significance. Anyone carrying out a business forecast risk assessment needs even more tact and diplomacy than when simply assessing the cost or schedule of a single project.

In spite of the added human complexity, risk modelling offers the same benefits to business forecasting as it does to project planning. It enables you to use the information you already have about uncertainty in the various parts of your business, to obtain a realistic view of the uncertainty in the enterprise as a whole. It provides a sound basis for setting and assessing targets, and a framework within which to evaluate options for improving your prospects.

6

ALTERNATIVE TECHNIQUES AND TOOLS

6.1 INTRODUCTION

This book offers a combination of useful ways to think about risk, and one particular way of analysing project-related risks quantitatively: Monte Carlo simulation. If you have gained some appreciation of these techniques and tools, you might want to look at some of the alternatives, to put those described here in context. This chapter gives a brief overview of some of the other techniques and tools you might encounter.

6.2 TECHNIQUES

The general approach to risk that underlies the preceding chapters has been developed on the job, so it is known to work. There are alternatives, and no one can say that any single method is right or wrong, only that some are more useful than others in certain situations.

Chapter 1 described scoring and issue-based assessment schemes, and outlined their strengths and weaknesses. A key factor that underlies the difficulties with these approaches to risk is the fact that they work in abstract terms. They register the presence or absence of an issue or an arbitrary score on a scale of 0 to 100 or similar. Monte Carlo simulation allows you to work in terms of real units like £ or weeks. This allows models to be firmly rooted in the plans of a business or project, and makes

129

the relationship between their output and real-world decisions relatively straightforward.

There is one method other than Monte Carlo simulation that works in real units; this is direct calculation of a project's overall uncertainty from that of its component parts. If you have distributions for all the separate costs of a project, then under certain conditions it is possible to calculate the distribution of the total cost. At first sight this might look attractive, but as you might expect there are pitfalls and problems.

Direct calculation is sometimes referred to as the method of moments. In statistical terminology the mean of a distribution is its first moment, the variance is its second, and there are other higher moments which are of little interest here. Direct calculation works by calculating the moments of the total distribution from the moments of its component distributions.

If you know the means of all your project's costs, then the mean of the total can be found by adding them up. Similarly, the variance of the total can be found by adding the variances of the components. With the mean and variance of the total cost, and drawing on the fact that the sum of a lot of distributions tends towards a normal distribution, you can estimate the range of likely total costs and the risk of exceeding any particular value in that range.

Being able to do all this without the overhead of a simulation would be attractive, if it were not for its limitations. The biggest limitations are that:

- it only works if there is no correlation between items

- it cannot handle uncertain events realistically

- it can only be applied to simple schedule models at best, and then only subject to the other two limitations.

If there is any correlation between the items in an analysis, the rule about adding variances together breaks down. You can formulate more complex rules to get around the problem, but they soon become unworkable. Risk assessment methods that rely on direct calculation generally require the analyst to break a project down in such a way that the parts are not correlated. This is not always easy to do, and it makes the analyst's task even harder than it would otherwise have been.

Uncertain events can be very important in projects, but it is impracticable to represent them in a direct calculation. This is not always an issue, but it crops up sufficiently frequently to represent a major problem if it is denied to you.

It is possible to write an equation for the overall duration of a set of uncertain activities in parallel or in series. Using building blocks of series and parallel groups of activities, a conventional network can be evaluated this way, although it is not a simple calculation. The fundamental problems arise when correlation becomes important or there are uncertain events, branching points, in the network.

These issues are discussed in a useful book by Hertz and Thomas (1983). The actual calculation stage of Monte Carlo simulation might appear difficult, but in fact it is just repetitive. Once that task has been automated for you by a simple tool like *@RISK*, building a simulation model is a relatively easy task, and one which is easily reduced to manageable-sized pieces of work.

6.3 TOOLS

6.3.1 The ones to avoid

There are several tools on the market that purport to offer project risk modelling capability, but are in fact seriously flawed. You can identify these by working through the following questions.

Can it represent the structures I want to model? No matter whether you are concerned with costs, schedules or related matters such as resources, you are likely to need to be able to represent both uncertain values and uncertain events. Look again at Chapters 2, 3 and 4 if you are not convinced. Overlaying everything you do, the matter of correlation is crucial to realistic modelling. So if a tool cannot handle uncertain events or makes no allowance for correlation, it is unlikely to be useful.

What is the user interface? The tools that operate within a spreadsheet, such as *@RISK* or Crystal Ball (which is described briefly below), have the advantage that a large part of their user interface is both easy to use and familiar to a large number of people. A few tools still operate through text file input and output, which requires the user to understand how information is to be organised, and possibly a set of special codes, the tool's language. This has a strong bearing on the speed with which a user can become proficient, and it can affect the take up of a tool by your target analysts. It is not unknown for the introduction of a new form of analysis to fail because the tool supporting it was disliked by those who had to do the work.

What is a typical run time? Run times are becoming less significant with each step forward in technology. However, there are still a few tools which are implemented in high-level languages, intended primarily as database management systems. These can run extremely slowly and they limit the number of iterations likely to be carried out in practice. Anything suffering from this problem is likely to have other shortcomings too.

If a tool passes these three simple checks it should do what you want, present few problems with introduction and operate satisfactorily. This all depends on you knowing what you wanted to do in the first place, of course. If you look to a tool to provide you with a risk management method and hope to avoid getting involved in uncertainty yourself, you are likely to be disappointed.

6.3.2 @*RISK* for Microsoft Project

The manufacturers of @*RISK*, Palisade Corporation, have recently released a version of the tool which works with Microsoft Project, the well known Windows-based project planning and control package. @*RISK* for Project allows users to define all the key parameters of a plan, such as durations and headcounts, as distributions, and then carry out a simulation of the plan to assess the range of outcomes that it could yield.

At the time of writing, the tool works in conjunction with Excel, so you need Excel, Project and @*RISK* to perform project cost and schedule risk assessments. It has the advantage of working with a proper planning tool which can handle the intricacies of network logic, relieving you of the need to construct network links manually in a spreadsheet.

The limitation of @*RISK* for Project derives from Microsoft Project itself. In common with all planning packages based on project control, it cannot represent uncertain events. Branching points in the network and uncertain step changes in the costs of activities cannot be represented directly. If the majority of your uncertainty derives from tolerances on your estimates, this restriction might not matter. In all other respects this version of @*RISK* is as capable as the original.

6.3.3 Crystal Ball

An alternative modelling tool which operates within Excel is Crystal Ball. Functionally it has a lot in common with @*RISK*, and all the models shown in this book could be implemented in Crystal Ball. However, it lacks some of the flexibility of @*RISK* and adopts a less direct mode of operation.

The differences between Crystal Ball and @*RISK* are derived from the way that distributions are set up. Instead of using the same syntax as other Excel functions, Crystal Ball holds the distributions in a separate area accessed through a special user interface. This makes it less straightforward to use existing spreadsheet values, such as a table of minimum, likely and maximum values, in a distribution in Crystal Ball, than it is in *@RISK*.

6.3.4 Predict!

Predict! is a stand-alone tool that offers a spreadsheet-type interface with comprehensive Monte Carlo modelling facilities. As with Crystal Ball, all the models shown in this book could equally well be built in Predict! It offers similar distributions, correlation mechanisms and formulae to link elements of a model with a full Monte Carlo simulation capability and graphical presentation of the results.

The factors which might weigh in the choice between Predict! and *@RISK* are the cost, which at the time of writing is more than *@RISK* and Excel put together, and the learning curve. The advantage of tools which use Excel is the large existing base of users who at least understand the basics of the spreadsheet tool. Against this, Predict! has more advanced post-simulation data analysis tools which might benefit some users.

6.3.5 Monte Carlo

The most capable and comprehensive project risk modelling tool on the open market is Monte Carlo, owned by Prima Vera and marketed through associated companies. It provides mechanisms to represent all the structures shown in this book and more besides. In addition to separate cost and schedule modelling, it can represent integrated cost-schedule models, taking account of resources and other constraints.

It is not surprising that with so much capability this tool is one of the more expensive, and it demands rather longer than the others to become proficient in its usage. Monte Carlo is a heavyweight tool for major projects, where the investment in the tool and the training necessary to use it can be justified by the high stakes.

REFERENCES

Brooks, F.P., *The Mythical Man-Month*, Addison-Wesley, 1974.

Hertz, D.B., and Thomas, H., *Risk Analysis and its Applications*, John Wiley & Sons, 1983 (reprinted 1984). ISBN 0 471 10145 1.

Kleijnen, J., and van Groenendaal, W., *Simulation: A statistical perspective*, John Wiley & Sons, 1992. ISBN 0 471 93055 5.

Turner, J.R., *The Handbook of Project Management*, McGraw-Hill, 1993. ISBN 0 07 707656 7.

INDEX

TITLES IN THIS SERIES